UNMANNED
AIRCRAFT

Brassey's Air Power: Aircraft,
Weapons Systems and Technology Series

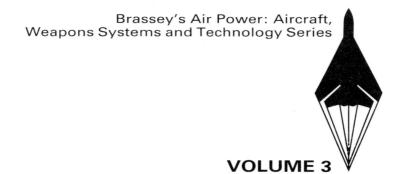

VOLUME 3

Brassey's Air Power:

Aircraft, Weapons Systems and Technology Series

General Editor: AIR VICE MARSHAL R. A. MASON, CB, CBE, MA, RAF

This new series, consisting of eleven volumes, is aimed at the international officer cadet or junior officer and is appropriate to the student, young professional and interested amateur seeking sound basic knowledge of the technology of air forces. Each volume, written by an acknowledged expert, identifies the responsibilities and technical requirements of its subject and illustrates it with British, American, Russian, major European and Third World examples drawn from recent history and current events. The series is similar in approach to the highly successful Sea Power and Land Warfare series. Each volume, excluding the first, has self-test questions and answers.

The early titles include:

Volume 1. Air Power: An Overview of Roles
AIR VICE MARSHAL R. A. MASON, CB, CBE, MA, RAF

Volume 2. Air-to-Ground Operations
AIR VICE MARSHAL J. R. WALKER, CBE, AFC, RAF

Volume 3. Unmanned Aircraft
AIR CHIEF MARSHAL SIR MICHAEL ARMITAGE, KCB, CBE, RAF

Electronic Warfare
AIR COMMODORE J. P. R. BROWNE, CBE, RAF

Air Superiority Operations
AIR VICE MARSHAL J. R. WALKER, CBE, AFC, RAF

Transport Operations
GROUP CAPTAIN K. CHAPMAN, MPHIL, BA, RAF

Air Defence
GROUP CAPTAIN M. B. ELSAM, FBIM, RAF

Brassey's Titles of Related Interest

C. CHANT
Air Defence Systems and Weapons: World AAA and SAM Systems in the 1980s

P. G. HARRISON *et al.*
Military Helicopters

R. A. MASON
War in the Third Dimension: Essays in Contemporary Air Power

B. MYLES
Jump Jet, 2nd Edition

P. A. G. SABIN
The Future of UK Air Power

UNMANNED AIRCRAFT

Air Chief Marshal Sir Michael Armitage, KCB, CBE, RAF

BRASSEY'S DEFENCE PUBLISHERS
(a member of the Maxwell Pergamon Publishing Corporation plc)

LONDON · OXFORD · WASHINGTON · NEW YORK
BEIJING · FRANKFURT · SÃO PAULO · SYDNEY · TOKYO · TORONTO

U.K. (Editorial)	Brassey's Defence Publishers Ltd., 24 Gray's Inn Road, London WC1X 8HR
(Orders)	Brassey's Defence Publishers Ltd., Headington Hill Hall, Oxford OX3 0BW, England
U.S.A. (Editorial)	Pergamon-Brassey's International Defense Publishers Inc., 8000 Westpark Drive, Fourth Floor, McLean, Virginia 22102, U.S.A.
(Orders)	Pergamon Press, Inc., Maxwell House, Fairview Park, Elmsford, New York 10523, U.S.A.
PEOPLE'S REPUBLIC OF CHINA	Pergamon Press, Room 4037, Qianmen Hotel, Beijing, People's Republic of China
FEDERAL REPUBLIC OF GERMANY	Pergamon Press GmbH, Hammerweg 6, D-6242 Kronberg, Federal Republic of Germany
BRAZIL	Pergamon Editora Ltda, Rua Eça de Queiros, 346, CEP 04011, Paraiso, São Paulo, Brazil
AUSTRALIA	Pergamon-Brassey's Defence Publishers Pty Ltd., P.O. Box 544, Potts Point, N.S.W. 2011, Australia
JAPAN	Pergamon Press, 5th Floor, Matsuoka Central Building, 1-7-1 Nishishinjuku, Shinjuku-ku, Tokyo 160, Japan
CANADA	Pergamon Press Canada Ltd., Suite No. 271, 253 College Street, Toronto, Ontario, Canada M5T 1R5

First edition 1988

Library of Congress Cataloging in Publication Data
Armitage, M. J.
Unmanned aircraft/Sir Michael Armitage. — 1st ed.
p.   cm. — (Brassey's air power: v. 3)
Bibliography: p.
Includes index.
1. Drone aircraft.   2. Cruise missiles.   I. Title.   II. Series
UG1242.D7A76   1988
623.74'69 — dc 19   88-22248

British Library Cataloguing in Publication Data
Armitage, M. J.
Unmanned aircraft.
1. Guided missiles
I. Title
623.4'519

ISBN 0-08-034744-4 Hard cover
ISBN 0-08-034743-6 Flexicover

The front cover illustration is an artist's impression of Teledyne Ryan AQM-34V 'Combat Angel' RPV (Teledyne Ryan Aeronautical)

Printed in Great Britain by A. Wheaton & Co. Ltd., Exeter

About the Author

Air Chief Marshal Sir Michael Armitage KCB, CBE has been Commandant of the Royal College of Defence Studies since January 1988. Before that he was responsible for all support functions in the Royal Air Force as Air Member for Supply and Organisation. His career also includes four years in senior Intelligence posts including that of Chief of Defence Intelligence in MOD LOndon. He has a varied background of flying, command, staff and academic appointments in the Service over a period of 41 years. He is author of *Air Power in the Nuclear Age* (with R. A. Mason) and is a writer and lecturer on defence, intelligence and air power topics.

Acknowledgements

The author is indebted to the following for their kind permission to reproduce copyright and other illustrations:

The Aerospace Museum, RAF Cosford: Fig. 3.1; The Brookings Institute: Fig. 6.6; Boeing Aerospace Company: Figs. 8.3 and 8.4; Canadair Ltd: Fig. 10.7; Development Sciences (Astronics Division, Lear Siegler Inc.) Fig. 10.5; GEC Avionics Ltd. Fig. 10.3; General Dynamics Corporation: Figs. 8.2 and 8.5; The Glenn L Martin Company: Fig. 5.1; Imperial War Museum: Figs. 2.1 and 3.2; Israeli Aircraft Industries Ltd: Fig. 7.15; Lockheed Corporation: Fig. 10.4; Macdonnell Douglas Corporation: Fig. 6.1; Mazlat (Israel): Figs. 7.12–7.14; The Ministry of Defence UK (Crown Copyright by permission of the Controller Her Majesty's Stationery Office): Figs. 6.3–6.8 and Fig. 6.10; Northrop Corporation: Figs. 10.1, 10.2 and 10.6; The RAE Farnborough: Figs. 1.1 and 1.2; Royal Swedish Air Force: Fig. 6.9; Salamander Books Ltd: Fig. 2.2; The Smithsonian Institution: Figs. 3.3–3.10 and Fig. 3.12; Teledyne Ryan Aeronautical: Figs. 7.1–7.6, 7.8 (and cover)–7.11; United States Air Force: Figs. 3.11 and 4.1; United States Navy: Fig. 5.2; United States Navy and Military Archive Research Service (MARS): Figs. 5.2, 6.1 and 6.2.

Contents

List of Figures

Introduction

Unmanned military aircraft can take several forms, but they are perhaps best defined as machines sustained in flight by aerodynamic lift over most of their path and guided without an on-board crew. They are, however, but one member of the wider family of vehicles exploiting the air for warlike purposes, and they are only one element in a wide and often overlapping range of platforms and weapons.

An illustration of the broad categories of aircraft and missiles is given in Figure 1, and a mention of the definitions the two main categories of unmanned aircraft, that is to say drones and remotely piloted vehicles, may also be useful at this stage. There seem to be no universally accepted definitions, but a drone can best be described as an autonomous and automatic pilotless aircraft. It will carry at least a mechanism to sustain stable flight, and it will either fly an uncorrected steady heading, in which case its only utility is likely to be as a target; or its course will be programmed in some way. An RPV, on the other hand, is a pilotless aircraft that transmits mission related data to a remote controller and reacts to his commands as well as to other control inputs.

One difficulty with all this is that some unmanned aircraft have the characteristics of both classes of machine, since they carry an automatic navigation and control system as well as a facility for remotely controlled over-ride. The reader should therefore expect to find some rather ill-defined boundaries between the various types of unmanned aircraft that are discussed in this volume.

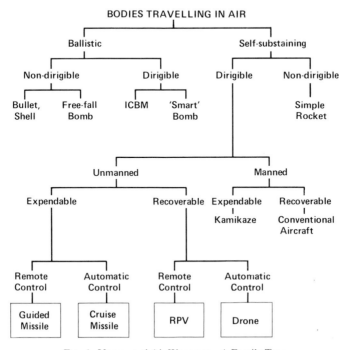

FIG. 1. Unmanned Air Weapons—A Family Tree.

Because of the sometimes uncertain boundaries that exist between definitions of missiles, glide-bombs and drones, and because of the influence that refinements in one type of device have had in the development of others, the approach adopted in this book is to deal with the more significant members of the whole family of unmanned airborne vehicles, including many that are, strictly speaking, missiles. The work does not claim to be a complete history, and it is certainly not a catalogue of all unmanned aircraft past or present. The approach adopted is, first, to give an account of the origins of unmanned aircraft, and then to trace the significant developments in the emergence of the first generation of unmanned aircraft during the first three decades of this century.

Next, the use of unmanned aircraft by the protagonists in the Second World War is discussed, and this covers the employment of the first operational cruise missile, the German V-1, as well as unmanned aircraft and such stand-off weapons as guided bombs, both free-fall and glide versions. The considerable post-war work on cruise missiles, notably in the United States, is then examined, and the decline of interest in these systems is explained as well as the subsequent revival of enthusiasm over their potential as developing technology made their attributes so much more attractive operationally. This is followed by an account of the convoluted emergence of the definitive US cruise missiles, before an account is offered of the activities of unmanned aircraft in the combat and near-combat conditions of the Far East and the Middle East.

Next a discussion is offered of the concepts within which unmanned aircraft find their place in modern air warfare, including the arguments on cost and effectiveness; and finally an analysis is made of the current state of the art of unmanned aircraft, and some thoughts are offered on their likely future utility.

In trying to cover such a wide historical, technical and international field, sources have not surprisingly proved to be of varied availability and reliability. At one end of the spectrum there are the Official Histories from which material has been drawn when treating US and British weapons systems, through to a large number of sometimes inconsistent secondary sources when dealing with, for example, the more esoteric German weapons of the Second World War, and down to informed speculation when dealing with episodes such as the Israeli employment of unmanned aircraft. Rather than use numerous specific footnotes therefore, the author offers a bibliography of the sources he has consulted.

Finally, the opinions offered here are those of the author only, and do not necessarily reflect the views of the Ministry of Defence or of the Royal Air Force.

1
Origins

Unmanned Aircraft have a history as long as that of aviation itself. Even before the First World War, a French artillery officer, René Lorin, had proposed the use of flying bombs to attack distant targets. These aircraft, he suggested, could be stabilised in flight by a combination of gyroscopes and a barometer, guided along track by radio signals from an accompanying piloted aircraft and propelled by a pulse-jet or a ram-jet engine to hit the target. This seems to have been one of the first attempts to design a weapon along the lines of such systems as the much later V1; but there were other and similar inventions by Victor de Karavodine and Georges Marconnet, also of France, although none of these early inspirations actually resulted in an aircraft being produced in that country or indeed anywhere else.

In Germany, work on guided missiles in the form of glide-bombs had been begun as early as October 1915 in the Siemens-Shuckert Werke. The experiments included several advanced features that were to come to maturity in the following decades, including servo-controls, which were operated in early models by batteries, but later by an airflow-driven generator. There was even a command guidance system that was operated by means of spooled copper-wires trailed out by the aircraft as it departed along its flight path, a development that seems to have been well ahead of its time. Although none of these early German systems was introduced operationally, by the time the armistice of 1918 halted work the experiments had advanced to include work on gliders of up to 2,205 lb weight with a range of about five miles, that had been launched from airships at Jutersborg.

The first live experiments with unmanned aircraft in the United Kingdom took place in 1917 when the Sopwith workshops, Geoffrey de Haviland and the Royal Aircraft Factory at Farnborough each produced simple pilotless aircraft using the newly designed 35HP ABC expendable aero-engine that had been developed by Granville Bradshaw. The Sopwith machine was abandoned before it flew, and the de Haviland machine seems to have met the same fate soon after; but Farnborough built six or more of their pilotless aircraft in mid-1917 and actually tested at least three of them at Northolt. These trials were the first to try to bring together the infant technologies of aerodynamics, light-weight engines and radio. The Northolt experiments involved launching the aircraft from a 50 foot horizontal ramp and up a 100 foot incline into free flight; but each machine in turn failed to meet the demands of the operator, as well as the hopes of the inventor, and stalled and crashed. With the end of the First World War in the following year, all experiments came to an end and most of the interest in the possibilities of unmanned machines abruptly fell away.

At about the same time as this activity was taking place in Britain, experiments had also been made along similar lines in the United States with what would be later called flying bombs, that is to say weapons that were self-contained, self-sustaining and unguided from the ground once launched.

Elmer Sperry of the Sperry Gyroscope Company, together with Peter Hewitt, successfully fitted and trialled an automatic control system in a Curtiss flying-boat in 1916. There was little interest in the experiment until the United States entered the war in April 1917, when funds were made available for further exploration of the idea of a flying bomb. In that same year, over 100 test flights were made by the five Curtiss N-9 seaplanes assigned to the programme, during which the aircraft were successfully monitored as they flew automatically towards the target before being recovered by the on-board pilot.

This encouraging progress then led to a United States Navy order for five aircraft, designed as flying bombs, from the Curtiss Company, but serious problems emerged when trials began at the end of 1917. The first two catapult launches quickly ended in crashes, and on the third the aircraft suffered engine failure. Further launches in early 1918 resulted in short flights, but it became clear that neither the catapult systems used nor the aircraft itself were performing satisfactorily. In order to identify the precise problems with the machine, a pilot was re-introduced into the aircraft and he discovered that the controls that had worked well in the Curtiss seaplane did not match the quite different aerodynamic characteristics of the flying bomb. Further adjustments and further tests were therefore made, this time with the flying bomb ingeniously mounted on a Marmon motor-car fitted with an OX-5 aircraft engine which drove the assemblage along at up to 80 mph, thus simulating the operation of a wind-tunnel. Even this failed, however, to resolve all the problems of the flying bomb, and after further failure had destroyed the remaining handful of machines, the programme was abandoned. Sporadic experiments continued towards the end of the war and after the Armistice, and although a number of short flights were made, the lack of progress and the cut in available funding as the United States Navy adapted to peace-time conditions, meant a sharp fall of interest in this type of weapon. Some experiments did, however, continue. Work was restarted on remote control by radio for unmanned aircraft in early 1921 with anti-aircraft targets for the United States Fleet, though this intitiative came to an end with further budgetary pressures in 1925. In 1935, a further attempt was made to introduce remotely-controlled anti-aircraft targets, partly as a result of the success in Britain of the Queen Bee aircraft.

The resulting target aircraft served to illustrate the very poor standard of gunnery in the United States Fleet rather than any outstanding success in the field of unmanned flight, but it was a sufficiently impressive performance by the aircraft to raise proposals for its use as an attack drone. This suggestion, though by no means novel, was given added impetus, first, by the development at about this same time in 1937 of airborne TV, which had been produced by RCA in an airborne reconnaissance project for the Soviet government; and second, by the development of the radio altimeter. Despite this, however, and under continuing pressures on funding, only sporadic progress was made by the American Navy with unmanned aircraft in the later pre-war years. It was not until the entry of the United States into the Second World War, that real enthusiasm was rekindled.

In parallel with the attempts by the Americans to develop a flying bomb, the interest of the United States Army had been aroused by the successful demonstration of automatic flight by an N-9 seaplane over a course of seven miles in November

1917. As a result, Charles Kettering, later to become President of General Motors, was given a contract to develop an unmanned aircraft. The result was a small, cheap and rather crudely-built biplane, which had a very pronounced dihedral of 10° to give strong lateral stability, and which was powered by a conventional 4-cylinder engine and a puller propeller. The official name of the aircraft was the 'Liberty Eagle', but it quickly attracted the sobriquet of 'Kettering Bug'. Twenty-five of the machines were ordered in January 1918, but the first—and manned—flights were not made until July. After three of these manned flights, experiments were made with the unmanned version launched from a trolley mounted on rails rather like tramlines. A mixture of successful flights and crashes then followed, but the successes were enough to persuade the Army Air Corps to order a further 75 copies of the machine. By now, however, the war was coming to an end and although experiments continued, the project was wound down at the end of November with only 20 of the Bugs completed. These examples of the aircraft were used in late 1919 for a series of further test flights in which out of 14 launches, ten ended in crashes and the best result obtained was a flight of only some 16 miles.

With these experiments, the Kettering Bug was abandoned, but interest in the United States Army Air Corps continued. In 1920, further experiments were made, this time with gyro-controlled automatic systems by Sperry fitted to three Standard E-1 and five Messenger aircraft. By late 1921, good results were being obtained with three of the Messenger aircraft fitted with upgraded control equipment. Further progress towards accurate direction for the flying bombs was demonstrated in mid-1922, when remote radio-control equipment was added to the project. Despite continuing problems of unreliability, which dogged the whole programme throughout its life, radio control experiments were continued on small scale until 1927. In that year, two aircraft were purchased specifically for further trials of remote control by radio, a Curtiss Robin and a Stimson Junior. Both aircraft proved, however, to be unsatisfactory in the role. This, combined with a growing stringency of funding, led to the demise of the programme and to the temporary end of interest by the United States Army Air Corps.

In Britain, too, sporadic interest continued after the war among a handful of enthusiasts and, as early as 1920, proposals for three types of inexpensive unmanned aircraft were being examined. One type was to be an 'aerial torpedo'. This would be launched from an aircraft and then radio-controlled by an operator in the parent aircraft for the 10 miles or so of its intended flight path. This forerunner of many developments that emerged some 30 or more years later was, however, abandoned in favour of more promising experimental effort that was being shown in two other concepts.

One of these was to be a 'munition carrier' which, after launch, was intended to fly a set heading, controlled by a gyroscope, over a pre-determined distance at a set speed. A third type was to be an aerodynamically stable machine designed to act as an aerial target and to have a range of 20 miles. Neither type was radio controlled. In the event, some of the features of each of these two concepts were combined into a machine known as the RAE (Royal Aircraft Establishment) 1921 Target, a machine with a wingspan of 23 ft, a length of 18 ft and an all-up weight at launch of 630lb including a warhead of 200lb. The aircraft was powered by a Siddeley-Deasy 45hp Ounce engine and was designed to fly at 6,000 feet with a speed of around 100 mph.

Trials with the RAE 1921 Target took place during 1922 and 1923 from tracks on the deck of the aircraft-carrier HMS *Argus* and from a launch-ramp on the destroyer HMS *Stronghold*, but they proved to be disappointing. Two launches from HMS *Argus* each resulted in an early nose-dive into the sea; and four launches from HMS *Stronghold*, made at a higher speed, produced flight-paths that were beyond the capacity of the on-board gyroscope to stabilise. Only the skilled responses of a pilot seemed capable of overcoming the limitations of a relatively crude and capricious gyroscope system. It was therefore decided to fit radio control to the RAE 1921. The result this time was a successful launch followed by a sustained and controlled flight that came to an end only when the engine stopped after twelve minutes. By the tenth flight in this series of experiments, an airborne duration time of 39 minutes had been attained, during which 43 separate radio command signals had been made by the controller and carried out by the aircraft.

This success led to the design of a more advanced production aircraft, which, because it produced a stable initial flight path, could now dispense with radio control. This machine was powered by a 200hp Armstrong-Siddeley Lynx engine and it proved able to carry a 250lb war-load over a range of 300 miles at what was then the very high speed of 193 mph. It was given the extraordinary designation of Larynx, a name derived from 'Long-Range Gun with Lynx Engine'. The aircraft is illustrated at Figure 1.1. Twelve of these machines were built at RAE Farnborough, and after some early disappointments with the first two of them, the feasibility of the Larynx

FIG. 1.1. Larynx No. 3 on HMS *Strongpoint*. (*Photo: RAE Farnborough. Crown copyright*)

was demonstrated when the third model, launched from a catapult from HMS *Stronghold*, completed a planned route over the sea along the coasts of Somerset, Devon and Cornwall.

After these successes it was decided to test the Larynx with a live warhead, and five of the remaining six aircraft were shipped to RAF Shaibah near Basrah at the head of the Persian Gulf, where the open desert offered ample margin of error for experiments with so rudimentary a weapon. The first launch of the armed Larynx was a failure, but the next three produced successful though short-lived flights. On the fifth attempt, however, the aircraft flew out into the open desert under the control of its automatic pilot, disappeared and was never recovered. One wonders whether astonished nomads ever chanced upon the machine, or whether it still lies undiscovered in the sand.

After these experiments, work on unmanned aircraft in Britain focussed again on radio-controlled machines and in particular on radio-controlled target aircraft. The first effective machine and the first practical demonstrations involved, not aircraft designed specifically for the role of targets, but instead they employed a version of the Fairey IIIF reconnaissance float-plane. This solution to the requirement emerged from a dispute between the Royal Air Force and the Royal Navy about the vulnerability of capital ships to attack from the air. The Royal Navy insisted that ships that were not only armoured and armed but were also capable of high speed evasive manoeuvre were unlikely to be easy targets for the limited loads of inaccurate bombs carried by contemporary aircraft. It was the aircraft, claimed the naval experts, that would be vulnerable in such circumstances.

Clearly some demonstrations were called for, and it was decided to modify three Fairey IIIFs to act as target aircraft (Figure 1.2). They would be fitted with a

FIG. 1.2. Fairey Queen IIIF Mark IIIB. (*Photo: RAE Farnborough. Crown copyright*)

radio-control mechanism, and the mainplane dihedral was increased to 10 degrees so as to give the aircraft the better lateral stability that would be demanded of a pilotless machine. Although these 'Fairey Queens' as they were christened were successfully test-flown carrying a pilot, the first two unmanned launches from catapults on HMS *Valiant* on 30 January and 19 April 1932 both resulted in crashes almost as soon as the aircraft were launched.

On 14th September, however, the third aircraft made a successful nine-minute flight, and it was later taken out to the Mediterranean by the Home Fleet for use during its Spring Cruise. The machine was duly launched to give the Fleet the opportunity to show the effectiveness of its anti-aircraft weapons and after surviving over two hours of heavy gunfire, it was safely landed again by remote control on the water. It finally succumbed to naval gunners some four months later. Meanwhile, not only had the inadequacy of naval anti-aircraft weapons been demonstrated, but so had the undeniable feasibility of remotely piloted aircraft. One result was that Specification 18/33 was drawn up in the following year, a move that lead to the design of the radio-controlled target version of the Tiger Moth biplane trainer, the Queen Bee, an all-wooden expendable airborne target. Between 1934 and 1943 no fewer than 420 of these machines were built to act as targets for the Royal Navy and for the British Army, but although they were relatively inexpensive, these aircraft were certainly not cheap. It must also be recorded that the fact that nearly all of them rendered very valuable service before being destroyed says more about the state of contemporary anti-aircraft defences than it does about the resilience of the Queen Bee aircraft.

2

Emergence — The V1 Weapon

Meanwhile, in those same years between the two World Wars, experiments with unmanned aircraft continued both in the United States and in Germany. In the latter country, the re-armament programme that began in 1933 grappled with the challenge of creating a war-fighting potential from a very slender economic base, and the scale of the development work that was undertaken by German scientists and engineers on less conventional weapons was therefore relatively modest. Nevertheless, among the areas of experiment in which the German Army and the newly-emerged Luftwaffe showed an early interest were those of pilotless missiles and of simple, inexpensive engines. One of these engines was the impulse duct or pulsating athodyd type that had originally been developed and patented in France in 1907.

DEVELOPMENT

By 1940, at least three greatly improved variations of this basic engine design had been separately evolved in Germany by Paul Schmidt of Munich, and by Dr Ing Fritz Gosslau of the Argus Motorenwerk. When it came to practical applications, attempts to fit the new motors on to heavily laden conventional aircraft so as to act as take-off boosters, proved less than successful, but General Milch, who was responsible for the equipment programme of the Luftwaffe, imaginatively recognised their potential in a quite different field, that of power units for air-breathing missiles. It was this novel application of the *Schmidtrohr* impulse duct engine that would lead ultimately to the first successful operational cruise missile and the first operational weapon to be propelled by any form of jet-propulsion, the V1 Flying Bomb (Figure 2.1).

After the defeat of the Luftwaffe in the Battle of Britain, and after the day and night bombing offensive against London had also been brought to a standstill, there was concern among the German leadership to maintain some kind of air threat against the United Kingdom while preparations were made for the invasion of Russia. The idea of using the fledgling German missiles, on which development had gradually proceeded, was seen to offer not only a means of intensifying the German effort in the air war against Britain, but also of doing so with a relatively simple weapon and above all, without risking the loss of scarce and highly trained aircrews. By 1942, with the enthusiastic support of Hitler and Goering, the aircraft designer Robert Lusser had drawn up the plans for what became the *Vergeltungswaffe Eins* (V1) known at the time by the codename of the *Kirschkern* (Cherry-stone) project within the *Vulcanprogram*, an umbrella name for most of the advanced projects being undertaken by the Luftwaffe at that time.

7

FIG. 2.1. V1 Flying Bomb launch. (*Photo: IWM*)

On 19 June 1942, Milch instituted development of the new weapon at the Luftwaffe experimental station and proving ground on the island of Usedom in the Baltic (a site more usually referred to as Peenemünde West) where ample range facilities were available over the sea. By the end of 1943, although the strength of the Luftwaffe had been steadily increasing, its expansion was on a far smaller scale than that of the Allied air forces by now being ranged against it, and what Hitler by this time saw not only as a failure in performance, but even as a breach of loyalty by the Luftwaffe, led him to put more and more faith in the development of secret weapons such as missiles. The V1 programme was therefore accelerated.

The V1 weapon itself (Figure 2.2) was a simple unmanned aircraft weighing just under 5,000lb at launch with a wingspan of about 19 feet and an overall length of almost 26 feet. The fuselage, which contained the warhead, the fuel and the autopilot mechanism, had a length of just over 24 feet and supported the dorsal-mounted Schmidtrohr type engine which had a length of about 12 feet. Early models of the V1 carried a warhead weighing 1,870lb over a range of 150 miles, but the standard versions had a warhead of 1,000lb and a range of 200 miles. Guidance in azimuth was provided by a gyroscope governed by a magnetic compass carefully pre-set before launch in a special building of non-magnetic construction. Height was controlled by an aneroid barometer which held the missile at about 1,000 feet or less over the ground, and range was governed by a propellor driven air-log which commanded a steep dive when the pre-set distance had been flown. The speed of the missile, at just under 400 mph, was less than the designer had hoped for, but it was a considerable achievement nevertheless and meant that the flight time of the weapon from launching sites in France to the target area in London would be very short.

It was true that the weapon lacked the accuracy to attack targets other than large

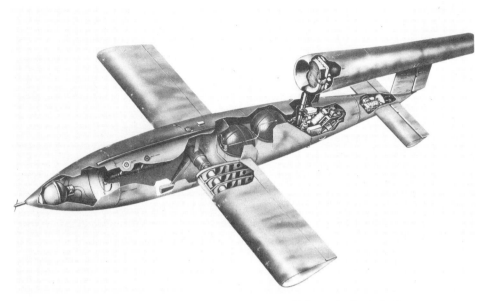

Fig. 2.2. Construction of the V1. (*Courtesy of Salamander Books Ltd*)

centres of population; but since it was explicitly designed for use as a retaliation for what the Germans saw as terror-bombing by the Allies, its relative inaccuracy and thus the unpredictability of its fall could actually be counted an asset. One other characteristic worthy of note was that when the air-log of the weapon operated the elevators to command a dive, this had the incidental effect of starving the motor of fuel. The missile thus made a dive to ground without any great kinetic energy, and the resulting shallow penetration before detonation meant that very heavy blast damage was caused if, as intended, the missile fell into a built-up area.

Although V1 production was given a high priority, there were numerous delays in the programme caused by technical, political and inter-Service factors. Nevertheless, in the first week of August 1943, and even before the weapon had been developed beyond the point at which a third or so of all launches were still failures, preliminary work was begun in northern France on the first operational launching sites with the intention of opening the campaign of bombardment against the British Isles on 15 December 1943. The plan was to start the initial attack two hours before dawn with a concentrated barrage of 300 missiles, codenamed *Grosses Wecken* (massive reveille), followed by a wave of missiles at noon, (*Salut*), or alternatively by harassing fire until evening when a *Grosser Zapfenstreich* (Grand Tattoo) of rapid fire would be launched to conclude the day's proceedings. On 16 August 1943, *Flakregiment* 155(W) was formed to operate the new weapons, and training for all the operators in the firing batteries began in the area of Peenemünde.

Further development and production delays intervened, however, and it was not until 21 October 1943 that the 1st Battalion of *Flakregiment* 155(W) entrained for the sites in northern France, where they were to assist in the final preparations for the initial launch. Another delay was then caused by the unwitting intervention on the night of 22/23 October of Bomber Command, which attacked Kassel, the home of the Fiesler works, and demolished the workshops that had just completed tooling up for V1 production. It was to be another three months before output could begin.

LAUNCH

Meanwhile, the work of constructing the launching sites was pressing ahead in France. The first two sites were huge bunkers containing underground chambers 625 feet long, 48 feet wide and protected by 15 feet of overhead reinforced concrete; but these were abandoned in favour of dispersed sites which were now built in a belt some 10 to 20 miles deep and 10 miles back from the coast, all the way from Flanders down to an area just north of Rouen. These sites were all aimed at London, but other sites were constructed in the Cotentin peninsula from whence attacks on the West of England could be launched. Construction of the first of the 64 main and 32 reserve launching sites, as well as eight major supply depots began in the first week of August and, within a fortnight, about 40,000 workers were engaged in what had become a huge programme of construction. Further production and technical problems, notably with the auto-pilot system were now encountered, however, and the German High Command was obliged once again to delay the planned start of the offensive.

The accumulated delays in the V1 programme meant that the planned attack on London had still not begun by 6 June 1944 when the Allied invasion of Normandy was launched; and since many senior Germans, including Hitler, were convinced that Normandy was a preclude to, or a feint away from, an invasion of the Pas de Calais, the very area in which so many V1 launching sites were deployed, a new start date was urgently fixed for 12 June. Despite enormous difficulties, including the logistic ones of transporting the missiles from Germany along routes that were under heavy Allied air attack, most sites were made ready in time. Such attacks as had been made by the Allies on the sites themselves had proved largely ineffectual.

The initial scale of the bombardment was, however, a serious disappointment to the German High Command. Instead of the expected massed launch of 500 Flying Bombs, a mere 10 missiles were dispatched when firing finally began on 13 June. This unpromising start led to the attack being called off to allow further preparations to be be made, and the offensive finally began in earnest three days later. This time 244 VIs were despatched from 55 of the launching sites, and although 45 missiles failed in the very early stages of their flight paths, 144 of the new weapons crossed the English Coast on that day and 73 of them fell into the London area.

By this stage of the programme, the production rate of VIs had risen to about 3,000 per month, and the German High Command expected to maintain the flying bomb offensive at about 100 missiles a day. But the logistic support for the weapons involved moving them from factories in Germany over the Belgian railway system into huge special storage caves in the valley of the Oise, and thence into forward storage sites. With this long supply route, any sharp increase in the daily firing rate was likely to be followed by a pause in the smooth supply of weapons, but, in spite of the break that this entailed in what was meant to be a steady bombardment, the rate of fire was increased from time to time, the first occasion being on 20 and 21 July after the abortive attempt on Hitler's life when 193 weapons were fired on the first night and over 200 more on the second. The maximum sustained rate of fire occurred during the first week of July when 800 flying bombs were launched. The offensive was at such a pitch by this time that, by mid-July, a total of about 3,000 of the bombs had come within range of the British anti-aircraft defences.

ALLIED ATTACKS

As early as November 1943, it had been recognised by the Allied Intelligence staffs that the new weapons that had been identified under test at Peenemünde might be launched in earnest against targets in the United Kingdom as soon as the associated launching sites in France were completed. The Allied response had taken the form of relatively small-scale bombing attacks by Boston and Mitchell aircraft using 500 and 1,000lb bombs. New photographic cover was flown on 3 December 1943 of the whole of France within 140 miles of Portsmouth and London so as to locate hitherto undetected launching sites, and as a result 27 of the sites were attacked, first in daylight on 5 December by USAAF Marauders and by rocket-firing Hurricanes, and then—less successfully—by night, using aircraft from units in Bomber Command.

By 14 December, the number of identified sites had risen to 69 and the difficulty of neutralising them, particularly in the face of very heavy defences, led to the adoption of new techniques, one of which, incidentally, involved dive-bombing by Tempest aircraft armed with two 500lb bombs. In a simultaneous effort to neutralise the sites and to inhibit the construction of any more, 672 B-17s of the 8th United States Air Force made an attack on 24 December against 24 sites dropping 1,400 tons of bombs. As a result of all these and earlier efforts, over 3,000 tons of bombs had been dropped on the launching sites by the end of that month. The disappointing fact was, however, that these not inconsiderable attempts to neutralise the threat at the firing points had destroyed only seven launching sites and severely damaged another 14.

All the same, the massive and growing weight of Allied bombing potential caused the Luftwaffe to reconsider the likely future vulnerability of the launching sites, and these very visible and obvious targets were abandoned in favour of simplified sites designed, sited and camouflaged in such a way that they were extremely difficult to detect and to identify. Nevertheless, on 27 April 1944, Allied photographic reconnaissance revealed what was found on examination to be a single launching ramp in the Cotentin peninsula, with its alignment on Bristol. This discovery then led to a complete and very detailed survey of the coastal region from Calais to Cherbourg, a search that resulted in the identification of 20 of the new sites by 13 May. As the Germans had intended, these sites were, however, to prove very difficult to attack and to destroy, particularly in the face of the increasingly dense anti-aircraft defences that were deployed to protect them.

At the same time, air attacks were being made against the sources of manufacture of the missiles and against the transportation and storage infrastructure that was to support their deployment and operation. During May 1944, for example, the USAAF 8th Air Force and the second Tactical Air Force of the Royal Air Force flew 3,000 missions in intensive attacks against the transportation systems in France and Belgium. This pattern of attacks on targets in France continued throughout the Summer of 1944, with some shift of emphasis to targets further from the coast from 20 June onwards once the principal storage sites for the V1s had been identified by photo-reconnaissance.

FURTHER COUNTERS TO THE V1

Considerable anti-aircraft and fighter assets were, of course, already to hand in the United Kingdom as a counter to attack by German conventional aircraft and, in the early stages of the V1 offensive, these defences shot down about 10 per cent of all incoming V1s over the sea. About half the remainder were brought down after they crossed the coast by fighters, anti-aircraft guns or barrage balloons. The balance, however, got through to the London area causing very considerable physical damage and great public alarm.

This very unsatisfactory situation led to a redeployment of the defences in the South of England in mid-July, when it was decided that all anti-aircraft guns would move forward into a concentrated belt on the South Coast so that the fighters would have a clear run over Southeast England as well as over the sea ahead of the gun line. By the morning of 19 July, 412 Heavy guns and 768 Light guns, British and American, as well as numerous smaller weapons, such as 20mm close engagement guns were in position and controlled by radars that had been carefully sited on high ground. A further 208 Heavy guns and 578 Light guns were deployed in the Thames estuary and between Blackwater and Whitstable to meet a new but anticipated aspect of the threat which emerged on 9 July, when flying bombs released from Heinkel IIIs based in Holland launched attacks on London from the East rather than from a South Easterly direction. The result of these defensive redeployments was a reduction in the number of kills by fighters, whose operating area had been split in two by the new gun line, but a steady climb in the number of kills by the guns, whose victims fell, as intended, into a 10 mile strip of more or less open countryside just behind the gun-belt.

The problems faced by the defences were, however, never fully overcome. Flying at nearly 400 mph, the total flight time for the V1 missiles along the 130 mile route from France to London was only some 22 minutes, a factor that called for extremely rapid defence reaction. Not only that, but because of the guns and the barrage balloons that were deployed just to the South of London, the fighter aircraft had an overland belt of only about 45 miles in which to operate. The high rate of travel of the V1 meant that even Spitfires specially modified to give them a little more speed found it difficult to carry out successful interception within this narrow area. The second problem was the sheer density of the attack once the Germans had ironed out the early problems of their new weapon. Most missiles tended to coast-in somewhere on a narrow front of only some 60 miles, greatly compounding the difficulties of the defence in tracking each and every intruding flying bomb. Although by mid-July the defences had managed to reduce the number of V1s reaching London from about 70 a day to 25, the weight of these indiscriminate attacks was still very considerable and their effect on the population a very serious and worrying one for the British Government.

In the continuing Allied air attacks against the Continent, up to half of the available bomber effort in the United Kingdom was by now being diverted against what were known as the 'Crossbow' targets, that is to say targets associated with the V1 and with the emerging V2 weapon. But the results achieved were still very disappointing. This led to such widespread dissatisfaction that a Joint 'Crossbow' Target Priorities Committee was set up, holding its first meeting on 21 July. The consequence of this was a decision to switch from the existing ratio of 3,000 tons of bombs against launching sites and less than 800 tons against production and storage facilities, to one in which 2,000 tons were dropped on the latter and 800 on the launching sites.

With this new balance of attack, a general offensive against all known Crossbow targets was launched in early August, and by early September 1944 the total weight of deliveries against Crossbow targets amounted to 118,000 tons. Of this, 98,000 tons had been directed against targets associated mainly with flying bombs. However, the fact was that even this major diversion of air effort was unable to neutralise, but only to harrass and to delay, the continuing launch of V1s against their targets in the United Kingdom.

GERMAN REFINEMENTS

During the offensive, the German High Command was naturally concerned to monitor the success or otherwise of their efforts to direct the weapons specifically against London in accordance with the wishes of the Führer. The first method attempted was to fit a small radio transmitter to one missile in every ten or so. The transmitter had a two-fold purpose; first its emissions were used to plot the early stages of the flight of the weapon, so that any necessary corrections, for instance to allow for shifts in the wind, could be applied to the following missiles. The transmitter then switched itself off until the bomb was about 35 miles from its intended point of impact, when it started up again. This final transmission was intended to be picked up by three High-Frequency Direction Finding stations which would be able to plot the final minutes of the missile's flight. The point at which the radio transmissions finally ceased would be the point of impact. The system did not, however, become fully operational. One of the D/F sites was put out of action by American bombers six days before the Normandy landings, and a second was captured by the Allies on the next day. Although the third station was able to give bearings and a distance run based on the flight time of the missiles, it could not give the accuracy of fix at impact that had been hoped for.

A second attempt to plot the impact points of the missiles was then made by modifying the transmissions of Freya radars to stimulate and then to receive the transmissions of a small IFF type of transponder fitted to some of the weapons. But as soon as these emissions began they were jammed by transmitters prepared by No. 70 Wing of the Royal Air Force in readiness for just such an eventuality.

From the plots that they did have, the German Command calculated that the mean point of impact of the missiles fired during the first few days of the offensive was located in South East London and that the CEP, the Circular Error Probable, was about seven miles, that is to say half the weapons were falling in an area of seven miles radius centred on the mean point of impact (MPI), Figure 2.3. But because this information was not conclusive enough the German High Command awaited the first reports from their agents in the London area. In fact, the very few German agents that there had been in the United Kingdom had all been compromised, and the main double agent working for the British now sent reports to Madrid for onward transmission to the German High Command stating that the V1s were overshooting the aiming point by several miles. Although this intelligence conflicted with the plots

Plot of Median points of V-1 impacts for nine one week periods,
30 June – 1 Sep 1944. The ★ symbol locates Tower Bridge,
the German aiming point.

Fig. 2.3. V1 Impact Points.

that were available, it was accepted by LXV Korps, the controlling headquarters, and the range was progressively shortened, with the result that the mean point of impact of the V1s, instead of being Tower Bridge in Central London as intended, moved steadily South East and then East, finally finishing up near Bexley.

This deception by Military Intelligence in Britain was threatened with compromise on one occasion when it was realised that obituary notices in the London newspapers could by used to make a crude plot of MPIs. Seventy notices in *The Times* for example indicated an MPI at Streatham Hill, and another 80 in the *Telegraph* produced an MPI at Clapham Junction. Newspaper censorship was therefore tightened so that deaths were not publicly attributed to enemy action, and the potential leak of intelligence was thus stopped.

While the early stages of the V1 offensive had been under way, the Germans had also been conducting trials, again in the Peenemünde area, to launch VIs from aircraft. Indeed it was one of these missiles which, because of overfuelling, exceeded its planned range and landed on the Danish island of Bornholm, where it was examined and photographed by Danish officials before the German authorities arrived to recover the wreckage. The results were then sent to London, where this first hard evidence of the rumoured pilotless aircraft had been put before the Defence Committee on 30 August 1943.

The concept of air-launched V1s seems to be been inspired by the need to maintain the V1 offensive in the event that the launching areas in Northern France were neutralised by an Allied invasion where Hitler expected it, that is to say in the region of Dieppe. It was hoped by the Germans that in this event air-launched missiles would be able to continue the offensive until technical developments made it possible to ground-launch the weapons from further to the rear. Extensive trials were carried out in the Baltic—and detected by British intelligence—using various aircraft as launching platforms. The Heinkel III proved to be the most successful platform, with a V1 weapon fitted to a pylon carrier mounted under the starboard wing of a specially modified aircraft. The trials showed that once trained, the aircrew could launch the missile with much the same accuracy as that achieved from ground launching sites, and the failure rate of 16 per cent experienced in the trials was also found to be within acceptable limits.

The first air-launched attack against the British Isles was made on 9 July 1944, but it was recognised for what it was when the plotted tracks showed that the V1s could only have been launched from near the Belgian coast, an area that contained no ground launching sites. Between 18 and 21 July, fifty air-launched V1s were released by aircraft of III KG3, and 20 of them fell in London. All told, this Gruppe fired 300 V1s at London, another 90 at Southampton and 20 at Gloucester before the advance of the Allied armies through Belgium and Holland compelled the progressive withdrawal of the unit from its airfields at Beauvais-Tille, Venlo and Gilze-Rijen. After reorganisation and reinforcement, a new formation of aircraft, I KG53, then resumed the attack on London on 16 September using 15 He IIIs from an available force of some 75 aircraft, most of them operated and dispersed among the bases of Schleswigland, Leck, Eggebeck, Aalhorn, Hesepe, Varelbusch, Handorf, Wittmundhafen and Zwischenahn.

Scattered air-launched attacks continued during the rest of September, but without any concentration of effort because the radio beacons, on which the aircraft navigators relied for the precision launch of the missile, were being effectively jammed by the operations of No. 80 Wing Royal Air Force. At the same time, and to meet the new threat from the air-launched V1s, a substantial number of AA guns was redeployed to cover the coast between the Thames estuary and Yarmouth. In spite of the widely scattered paths along which the flying bombs could be launched, these guns destroyed more than half the incoming V1s before they crossed the coast; others were shot down by fighter aircraft from bases in East Anglia.

Two new methods were now tried by the Luftwaffe in their efforts to improve the accuracy of these air-launched attacks, one using the ground-based *Zyklop* navigation aid, and the second employing *Schwan* VHF marker buoys laid at sea by a pathfinder unit. Using these aids, and despite the worsening autumn North Sea weather, the offensive thus continued, with up to 20 Heinkel III aircraft taking part on the most active nights. On 24 December, a special effort was made involving 50 Heinkels, which at last made full use of the high flexibility available to them in the choice of launching area, and directed their attack against Manchester. Thirty missiles crossed the relatively undefended coast of Yorkshire, one falling in the city of Manchester itself, six falling within 10 miles of the aiming point and another eleven within 15 miles of it. As a result, some British anti-aircraft defences were once again redeployed, this time to cover the North East coast, but by now the Luftwaffe had shot its bolt and the last air-launched flying bomb fell on the North East outskirts of London on 14 January.

During the campaign, KG53 had launched a total of some 1,600 V1s against the UK, about one fifth as many as were fired from ground-launching sites in France. Of the 1,200 V1s launched by KG53 after 16 September, 638 were reported as crossing the coast of Britain, more than 400 were destroyed by the defences, 66 fell in London, one struck Manchester and another 168 fell in random fashion over the Eastern Counties.

There was to be one more brief phase of the campaign, starting on 3 March, during which 275 bombs were aimed at London, 125 of them flying close enough to the British coast to be observed and 87 of those being brought down by gunfire while another four were destroyed by fighters. Of the 34 missiles that eluded the defences, 13 reached the target area. The offensive against London finally ended with two bombs on 28 February. On the next day, the very last V1 to elude the defences fell in Kent, while the last one to approach the coast was engaged and destroyed offshore by guns at Orfordness.

During the offensive, 8,892 flying bombs had been launched from ramps and another 1,600 or so from aircraft. Of those, 1,847 were destroyed by fighters, 1,878 by guns and 232 by barrage balloons. 2,419 bombs reached the London Civil Defence region, causing casualties of 6,184 killed and 17,981 seriously injured. By comparison the figures for conventional bombing casualties in the United Kingdom during the whole war were 51,509 killed and 61,423 seriously injured. (The V2 rocket weapon campaign resulted in an additional 2,754 killed and 6,523 seriously injured.)

All told, Allied fatalities—both Service and civilian—attributable to the V1 offensive totalled 7,810. The physical damage caused was also very considerable. During the critical period of bombardment by V1 missiles and V2 rockets, as many as 50 factories were put out of action in one day in the London area, and of about 30,000 factories in the same area engaged in essential work, 919 were affected by missiles or rockets. By June 1944, 21,000 men were engaged on bomb damage repair work in the London Region, and by the end of October 6.5 million man-days had been absorbed in repairing damaged property, mainly houses.

There was also a 10 per cent reduction in productivity in the London area at the height of the campaign caused by time spent in shelters, absenteeism and a general drift away from the capital. By the third week of July, it was estimated that 530,000 people had made their own arrangements to leave London, and a month later it was estimated that no fewer than 1,450,000 people had left, 275,000 under official schemes. These were all very serious and disruptive consequences, both in terms of the war effort and in terms of social strain.

THE BALANCE

The V1 flying bomb had many potential advantages for the Luftwaffe. First, because it was constructed of thin sheet metal, propelled by a very simple motor and used only standard 75 octane MT fuel, it was a relatively cheap device. Contemporary estimates by the Royal Aeronautical Establishment suggested that a V1 manufactured in the United Kingdom would have cost only £115, or about £1,600 at 1988 prices. In fact, since V1 production depended very heavily on slave labour, particularly at the main factory of Mittlewerke near Nordhausen, this figure of £115 was likely to have been a considerable over-estimate. Second, with the possible exception of some of the autopilot components, the materials used in the construction of the missile put no undue demands on the limited German stocks of strategic materials. Third, and of obvious but crucial importance, the use of the weapon avoided the loss of scarce and expensively trained aircrew.

The V1 campaign had very wide ramifications, and it is of some interest that in November 1944 an attempt was made by the Air Ministry to quantify the relative cost of the campaign itself to the Germans, and the cost to the Allies. The only basis on which even the most crude and incomplete balance could be drawn was that of financial cost, but including the cost of resources such as manpower as well as materials. The result was an assessment that the campaign had caused the Allies to incur extra expenditure of £47,635,000 while the cost to the Germans was estimated to have been £12,600,000—a leverage of 4:1 in favour of the attack.

Seen in broader terms, this first campaign in which unmanned aircraft were used as weapons was, in direct military terms, nothing more than a nuisance. In terms of civilian morale, however, it was a very serious threat indeed. Apart from the efforts of the UK defences, which were deployed in any case, very extensive resources had to be devoted in attempts to neutralise the weapons at source and before launch, including some 93,000 tons of bombs that were dropped on V1 sites and factories. The losses sustained by Allied air forces in these attacks were very heavy, particularly in view of the meagre successes that were achieved. Nearly 450 aircraft were lost and 2,900 valuable aircrew lives were sacrificed. It may be true that the German High Command had not achieved anything like the success for which they had hoped, but the effect of these inexpensive and relatively simple weapons had nevertheless been little short of traumatic.

The development and deployment of the V1 and V2 weapons was part of a wider German emphasis on an air strategy of retaliation rather than on one of gaining air superiority, and although the remorseless and highly dangerous growth in Allied air supremacy was clear to some senior officers, notably General Milch and General Jeschonnek, Hitler himself held to his conviction that offensive weapons were the key to the air war, and less emphasis was put on constructing an effective defence against the allied air offensive over Germany.

Thus it was that, when faced in the summer of 1943 with a choice between a massive switch of aircraft production either into day and night fighters or into weapons of retaliation, the German High Command chose the latter—including the V2 in the case of the Army, and the V1 flying bomb in the case of the Luftwaffe. One of the indirect but vital consequences of the Allied strategy of area bombing was therefore that of diverting German production away from the sectors that might have succeeded in deflecting or diluting the Allied air offensive.

The V2 has not been dealt with here, since it will be described in the volume in this series by Air Chief Marshal Knight on Strategic Bombardment, but it is worth noting that although the V2 ballistic missile was a remarkable piece of engineering and innovation, it was also a very expensive device which, among other things, used raw materials that were in short supply. Furthermore, its production caused a major diversion of effort in the over-stretched electrical and instrument sectors of German industry. But ironically enough, because there was no practical defence against the V2 weapon, its use caused only a minor diversion of Allied war effort, notably in the efforts of Bomber Command and the United States 8th Army Air Force, a diversion that became even less significant because attacks on targets such as Peenemünde were of course designed to neutralise the V1 offensive at source as well as the threat from the V2s.

3

Unmanned Aircraft at War

GERMAN WEAPONS

The V1 offensive has been dealt with in some detail because of its interest as the first large-scale operational employment of unmanned aircraft. Nothing remotely comparable was attempted by any of the other combatants, but the V1 offensive was by no means the only use of unmanned aircraft during the Second World War either by the German armed forces or by the Allies.

If, as has been explained, we include all manner of glide-bombs in the category of unmanned aircraft, then one of the earliest—and certainly one of the most success-ful—operations with these particular weapons was the attack by the Luftwaffe against the Italian fleet in September 1943. On 9th of that month, the German unit III KG 100 based in the area of Marseilles and flying Dornier 217Ks, attacked the Italian battleships *Italia*, *Roma* and *Vittoria Veneto* which were sailing from La Spezia to surrender and join the Allied fleet. Using Fx-1400 *Fritz* radio-controlled glide-bombs (sometimes known as *Fritz* X, Figure 3.1) and HS 293 radio-controlled glide-bombs, (Figure 3.2) twenty-eight Do 217s took off from Istres near Marseilles to attack the Italian fleet in the Straits of Bonifacio. Before describing the effect of these glide-bombs in operations, it will be useful to deal with their technical characteristics.

The Fx-1400 was a 3,000lb armour-piercing air-to-ground guided bomb fitted with fins attached at the centre of gravity point, and with a cruciform tail extension containing a sighting flare and a radio-control receiver. This last was connected to spoiler-type elevators and rudders that moved directly in phase with radio pulses to guide the weapon during its fall. After release, a controller in the parent aircraft tracked the bomb by means of the flare, using a control stick to maintain the weapon on its sightline to the target. It was a cheap, simple and effective weapon, and designed to be released from between 6,000 and 7,000 metres in order to penetrate the armoured decks of the warships that were intended to be its targets. The other glide-bomb, the HS 293, was a miniature jet-propelled aircraft. Its two mainplanes were attached directly to the 550 kilogramme warhead, and the rear body contained the instrumentation as well as supporting a high-set tailplane. A group of five flares was fitted at the tail to make the weapon visible to the airborne controller during its flight. A Walter booster rocket was also fitted, designed to burn for ten seconds so as to give the missile an additional forward speed of 55 metres per second after launch.

This configuration not only made it possible to use the HS 293 in low-level attacks, but it also reduced the necessary exposure time of the parent aircraft, a fact that became very important when the Allies began to use radar to detect the attacking

FIG. 3.1. Fritz-X Glide Bomb. (*Photo: Aerospace Museum, RAF Cosford*)

FIG. 3.2. Henschel HS-293 being examined by an RAF officer in 1945. (*Photo: IWM*)

bombers. Like Fritz-X, this weapon was equipped with radio control, a sighting flare and control surfaces, but it was not an armour-piercing bomb, being intended for use against soft-skinned merchant ships. One second after release from the parent bomber, the rocket ignited and the weapon accelerated to a speed of between 120 and 250 metres per second, flying for between 25 and 80 seconds while the controller guided the bomb by line of sight onto its target. It could be released at a distance of between 3.5 and 18 kilometres from the target from heights between 400 and 2,000 metres, and it reached a maximum airspeed of 200 metres per second at the point of motor cut-off. Like the Fritz-X, the HS 293 had a hit probability of about 40 per cent in operations.

In the attack of 9 September, one of the Fx-1400s struck the Italian flagship *Roma*, and penetrated to the forward fuel tanks before exploding, causing the ship to blow up with the loss of 1,500 of the crew, including the Admiral. The *Italia* was also hit, but managed to reach Valetta Harbour in Malta. Versions of the same weapon were used a week later against the Allied invasion fleet at the Salerno landings. During these landings, the period from the 9th to the 16th September saw an extensive use of air power by both sides, and the particular results of the Luftwaffe effort with glide-bombs played a significant part in the operation as a whole.

On 11 September, one Fx-1400 glide-bomb scored a very near miss on the American cruiser USS *Philadelphia* badly shaking her, while another fell 15 ft away from the fleet flagship, the cruiser USS *Savannah*. A second weapon aimed at *Savannah* then hit her No. 3 turret and penetrated deep into the hull of the ship before exploding, causing very severe damage and killing more than one hundred members of the crew. *Savannah* was compelled to withdraw from the action, but she was able to make a successful passage back to Malta for repair.

In a further attack two days later, the cruiser HMS *Uganda* was hit by a glide-bomb which went right through the ship before exploding beneath her, causing such severe damage that she had to follow the other damaged ships back to Malta under tow. The destroyers HMS *Loyal* and HMS *Nubian* as well as the USS *Philadelphia* narrowly escaped being hit in these attacks, but the hospital ship *Newfoundland* was less fortunate and became a third casualty when she was struck by a glide-bomb, set ablaze and eventually sank. On 16 September, HMS *Warspite* was attacked with a salvo of 3 Fritz-X, one of which penetrated six decks and exploded against the double bottom, blowing a hole in it. One boiler room was demolished, four of the other five flooded and the ship took on 5,000 tons of water, putting her out of action until June 1944.

It was particularly noteworthy that the heaviest losses among the considerable Allied fleet operating off the coast of Italy had been caused by glide-bombs rather than by attacks using conventional air weapons. The difficulty for the Allied defence in dealing with these new weapons was that they were being released at around 6,000 metres, well above the height of effective anti-aircraft gunfire and too high to allow the Lightning fighters assigned to the defence of the fleet to climb and intercept the German weapon-carrying aircraft before they released their bombs and made off. As to evading the bombs themselves, their terminal velocity was in the order of 800 feet per second, far too rapid a fall to allow any ship the opportunity to take avoiding action.

The Allied landings at Anzio on 22 January of the following year led to a further series of German air attacks on an invasion fleet. Between 23 January and 3 February 3rd about 140 bombers of the Luftwaffe redeployed to Northern Italy from bases in Northwest Germany, France and Greece, while at the same time the German anti-shipping force in the South of France was reinforced with betweeen fifty and sixty additional Dornier 217s and Heinkel 117s equipped with radio-controlled glide-bombs. In various dusk and dawn attacks between 23 and 27 January, the Luftwaffe flew some 212 sorties against the ships off Anzio, many of the attacks employing the glide-bomb weapons. In these raids HMS *Janus* was sunk by an aerial torpedo, HMS *Jervis* was damaged by a glide-bomb, a United States destroyer, a cargo ship and a minesweeper were sunk, the hospital ship *St David* was hit and her sister ship the *Leinster* was set on fire. These were substantial results from so new a weapon in air warfare.

Apart from what seems to have been an experimental use of glide bombs in the Bay of Biscay against escort groups on 27 August 1943, which sank the sloop HMS *Egret*, the first ever sinking by an Air-to-Surface Missile, there seem to have been only three other noteworthy instances of the employment of glide-bombs in the European theatre of operations. The first was an attack against Plymouth during Allied preparations for the Normandy invasion on 30 April 1944, when fifteen specialist anti-shipping aircraft of *Fliegerkorps* X armed again with *Fritz*-X radio-controlled bombs attempted, without success, to attack major fleet units in the area. No other missions with these weapons in British waters are recorded.

The second took place during the Normandy invasion itself, when on 15 June 1944, Luftflotte III made air attacks on the Allied invasion fleet off the Normandy shore. Most of the Luftwaffe aircraft engaged carried the usual armament of conventional torpedoes; but some (the number is uncertain), were armed with *Fritz*-X weapons and others with HS 293 glide-bombs. However, the German air attacks were overwhelmed by the greatly superior Allied air effort in the area of the beach-heads, and the result was that during the critical first ten days of the invasion only five Allied ships were lost to direct air attack. The third, and apparently the final use of glide-bombs in Europe also took place during the campaign in Normandy. During the breakout by General Bradley's forces, on 1 and 2 August 1944, General Patton had seized key bridges over the rivers See and Selune at the town of Avranches and the village of Pontaubault respectively. Patton was able to move seven divisions down just one of these roads over a period of only 72 hours and the German Command, realising the threat, directed aircraft of Luftflotte III to destroy the bridges. Attacks were launched both by conventional bombers and by Dornier 217s carrying HS 293 glide-bombs in what seems to have been the first and only recorded attempt to use this type of weapon against land targets. In the event, the attacks were unsuccessful and during one forty-hour period, a United States Army Anti-aircraft Battalion in the area claimed to have shot down eighteen of the forty attacking German aircraft.

There were many other German experimental systems during the Second World War that fall into or near the definition of unmanned aircraft, including the experimental HS 294. This was a 20 foot long missile designed to glide into the sea after release, when its wings were jettisoned, allowing the body of the device to proceed towards the target as an acoustically-guided torpedo. Other weapons in the series, the 295, 296 and 298 were very much at the experimental stage by the end of the war, and none of them approached operational service.

Work in Germany on rocket motors and remote-control systems also led to the development of four anti-aircraft rockets known as *Wasserfall*, *Rheintochter*, *Enzian* and *Schmetterling*. Although, strictly speaking, these were not unmanned aircraft, their characteristics make them of some interest in the general field of remotely controlled and automatic weapon systems.

Wasserfall and *Rheintochter* were supersonic missiles fitted with stub wings in a cruciform cross-section; *Enzian* and *Schmetterling* were subsonic weapons with characteristics more like conventional aircraft. *Wasserfall* was actually derived from the V2 missile, and it was designed to destroy formations of bomber aircraft at medium altitudes as well as individual high-flying aircraft. The missile was to be guided to the vicinity of its target by radio command signals using the information from two radars, one following the target and the other following the missile, until the missile was within the effective range of its proximity fuse. By February 1945, about 35 trial launchings had been made with *Wasserfall*, and although it did not enter operational service, the experience gained by the German engineers later played a part in the development of the American Nike missile.

Schmetterling had its origins in the experience gained with the HS 293 glide-bomb. Two booster rockets and a liquid-fuelled main motor initially accelerated *Schmetterling* from its zero-length launcher to a high sub-sonic speed, the boosters were jettisoned after four seconds and the missile then continued its climb to the target guided by radio command signals. Large-scale production was begun before the end of the war, but this weapon, too, failed to enter operational service before the end of the conflict.

Rheintochter was a two-stage experimental radar-tracked anti-aircraft rocket. Eighty or so of these missiles had been fired by the end of the war, twenty with radio-guidance and most of them successfully. *Rheintochter* was also the basis used to develop the *Rheinbote*, a three or four stage surface-to-surface missile carrying a warhead of some 88 lbs. Over two hundred of these weapons were fired at Antwerp during the closing stages of the campaign in Northwest Europe, but they caused little damage and the war ended before the weapon could be refined to a more successful stage.

Together, the numerous German operational and experimental systems of the Second World War demonstrated ingenuity and innovation bordering on desperation, particularly in the later stages of the Third Reich. This innovative work embraced experiments with Television guidance for the HS 293 missile, referred to as the HS 293D, the only TV guided missile being tested by 1945, and it also included trials with high frequency homing devices for the *Fritz-X*. There was even some promising progress towards an effective infra-red homing system.

Rather further away from any prospect of operational deployment, but nevertheless noteworthy for their advanced concepts, were several other German projects for advanced missiles. One of these was the HS 298 air-to-air missile developed from the glide-bombs already described. This was a line-of-sight, radio-controlled weapon essentially of simple and robust design. Control of the missile about the rolling axis was provided by only one aileron instead of the conventional two, and there was a spoiler to give control in pitch in place of the more usual elevator. Power for the on-board radio was drawn from an air driven generator, a measure that dispensed with the need for heavy batteries and thus saved overall weight.

That particular version of the HS 298 was remotely controlled from a parent aircraft; but several more advanced versions of this and of other missiles were under active development by the end of the war, including some experimental systems in which the infra-red homing device could detect, and presumably lock-on to the target, before launch; and others in which the parent aircraft carried its own additional infra-red search devices, as well as others in which an infra-red proximity fuse was used to increase the probability of destroying the target aircraft.

Other experiments with air-to-air missiles included passive radar homing devices such as *Max P*, which was claimed to have an effective range of 50 kilometres against airborne radar transmitters, *Max A*, an active radar homing system, and a development of the *Fritz-X*, a wire-guided air-to-air missile known as X-4. Finally, and in yet another extension of the basic *Fritz-X*, a smaller version of the X-4 was developed for the anti-tank role. This was the X-7, again a wire-guided missile. None of these systems reached operational status before the war ended, but the results of the many German experiments in this and other related fields, as well as the scientists involved in the work, often found their way either to the United States or to the Soviet Union.

In all the German initiatives that have been described, the steps taken within very constrained resources towards the employment of viable unmanned aircraft and remote-controlled rocket systems were considerable, and it is interesting to note that they were driven by the three imperatives that still provide the stimulus in this field today: above all a search for better weapon to target matching, particularly in terms of accuracy; next, in attack the need to operate aircraft outside the range of highly effective terminal defences; and particularly striking, attempts to dispense with scarce and expensive aircraft crews altogether where that approach did not unacceptably degrade operational effectiveness.

UNITED STATES WEAPONS

Allied efforts to introduce unmanned aircraft during the Second World War included the development by the United States Army Air Corps and the United States Navy of Glide Bombs and of guided Vertical Bombs. Several models of each were produced. As early as 1940, experiments had been made with these air-to-surface weapons, but by 1942 only one, the GB-1 (Glide Bomb 1, Figure 3.3) showed enough promise to survive as a project. This weapon was a standard 2,000lb GP (General Purpose) bomb, but fitted with 12 foot wings and twin booms to carry the twin fins and the tailplane. The bomb was designed to be launched from about 15,000 feet at targets twenty miles away, thus enabling the launching aircraft to remain outside the terminal defences at the target. Although fitted with a simple autopilot, it was an unguided and therefore a grossly inaccurate device. But in 1944, the intensity and lethality both of German fighter air defences and of their Flak weapons—by now using radar prediction—had led to very serious concern about American bomber losses, and even so inaccurate a weapon solution could not be ignored.

April 1944 was a particularly bad month for the United States Army Air Corps. A sustained effort by the 8th Air Force had led to the loss of no fewer than 512 aircraft missing in action, and another 65 damaged beyond repair. Of that total, 361 aircraft

FIG. 3.3. GB-1 American Unguided Glide Bomb, launched from a B-17 Bomber. (*Photo: Smithsonian Institute*)

were heavy bombers (a loss rate of 3.6 per cent) and it was assessed that in 131 of those losses enemy anti-aircraft fire had played a part. This was double the number of losses for the preceding month. It was clear that the electronic jamming, using such techniques as Carpet, Mandrell and chaff, being employed by the Americans against the German gunlaying radar by this stage of the war, was inadequate to the challenge.

Flak did not claim as many victims in May as it had in April, but the unpleasant fact was that the extent and the density of German anti-aircraft artillery was still growing, and further counter-measures were clearly essential. The use of glide-bombs by the United States Army Air Corps was therefore reconsidered. The result was that aircraft of the three Groups of the 41st Combat Wing, that is to say the 303rd, 379th and 384th Bombardment Groups at Molesworth, Kimbolton and Grafton Underwood respectively, were fitted with wing racks to take the GB-1, each B-17 carrying two of the twelve-foot span weapons. On 28 May, the Wing flew a mission with the new bombs against the Eifeltor railway marshalling yard near Cologne, and 109 of the weapons were released. The results were disappointing. The accuracy of the bombs was so poor that, even against so large a target, the mission was less than successful, some of the bombs falling miles away from the area of intended impact. Although further raids using GB-1s were made during the following months, it was clear that a better weapon was needed if stand-off attacks were to have any effectiveness at all, and later versions of the bomb were therefore fitted with the means of improved accuracy, namely radio-controlled guidance.

In the case of one variant of the GB-1, the GB-4 (Figure 3.4), a weapon weighing 2,400lb, was fitted with a primitive TV camera so that the operator in the parent

FIG. 3.4. GB-4 American TV Guided Glide Bomb. (*Photo: Smithsonian Institute*)

FIG. 3.5. GB-8 American Radio Guided Glide Bomb. (*Photo: Smithsonian Institute*)

FIG. 3.6. GB-14 American Radar Homing Glide Bomb. (*Photo: Smithsonian Institute*)

aircraft could steer the gliding weapon down on to its target. However, the GB-4 did not prove to be a very robust weapon once it left the experimental ranges to be deployed on operational stations, and its employment was very limited. Other variations then followed in later months, including GB-6A, which carried an infra-red heat seeker, presumably intended to guide itself into fires on the ground; GB-8, (Figure 3.5) a visually controlled radio-guided version; GB-13, a light-seeking weapon designed to home on to a bright flare; and GB-14, (Figure 3.6) which became the first ASM to carry an active-homing radar guidance system; but none of these advanced versions of the original glide-bomb entered service before the end of the war.

In addition to that Glide-bomb family of weapons, the United States Army Air Corps was also working on the introduction of guided free-fall vertical bombs. These were existing conventional High Explosive bombs, but fitted with modified tail assemblies by means of which the weapons could be guided during their fall on to the target. Only one type was produced in numbers and used operationally. This was the first American guided vertical bomb, VB-1, named Azon (for Azimuth only) because it had guidance in azimuth but not in range (Figure 3.7). Azon was basically a standard 1,000lb M-44 bomb carrying a modified cruciform tail in which was mounted a tracking flare, a radio receiver and a gyroscope so as to keep the bomb steady in the vertical plane. Trials in the United States showed that the bomb was more accurate than the unguided version by a factor of 29, and the first batches of the

Fig. 3.7. American Radio Controlled AZON Bomb. (*Photo: Smithsonian Institute*)

FIG. 3.8. VB-3 American Radio Guided RAZON Bomb. (*Photo: Smithsonian Institute*)

bomb were delivered to the 15th United States Army Air Force in Italy. Here they were employed in successful attacks on the Danube locks at the Iron Gates in Hungary, and on the Avisio viaduct south of the Brenner Pass in Italy. Attacks were also made using Azon on 31 May 1944 against the Seine bridges by B-24 Liberators of the 458th Bombardment Group based at Horsham St Faith, but these were less successful and none of the 14 bombs released scored a hit on the target.

In the Far Eastern theatre of operations, better fortune attended a raid in Burma on 27 December 1944 when nine VBs brought down the rail bridge at Pyinmana, a target that had defied the efforts of numerous air attacks during the preceding two years. Other successes followed in the Burma theatre, with a score of twelve to fifteen per cent of all releases being direct hits against such targets as bridges out of all the 493 Azon bombs that were dropped during the campaign.

Later versions of the VBs were fitted with elevators, which controlled the glide-angle and thus the range, as well as with azimuth controls, although, like the later GBs, these weapons were introduced too late to be employed operationally during the war. The VB-3 (a 1,000lb weapon) (Figure 3.8) and VG-4 (a 2,000lb version), named Razon (Range and Azimuth), were among these later variants. Both bombs were similarly guided by flare and radio, and they were also stabilised by means of a gyroscope. VB-5 was a more advanced version consisting of a 1,000lb bomb guided by an image contrast light-seeking device, while VB-6 was another 1,000lb weapon (Figure 3.9), but this time fitted with an infra-red seeker-cell in the nose. This was a weapon which, in trials during 1945, demonstrated a CEP of 85 feet over 12 drops, VBs 9, 10, (Figure 3.10), 11 and VB-12 were further versions using radar, TV, IR and direct visual control respectively. The final VB, VB-13, (Figure 3.11) was, at a weight of 12,000lb. a very much larger and more destructive weapon. Named Tarzon, the weapon was a modified British Tallboy or earthquake bomb, 21 feet long and fitted with an annular wing 54 inches in diameter, together with a

Fig. 3.9. VB-6 American Infra-red Guided Vertical Bomb. (*Photo: Smithsonian Institute*)

Fig. 3.10. VB-10 American TV Guided Vertical Bomb. (*Photo: Smithsonian Institute*)

FIG. 3.11. VB-13 American Radio Guided Tarzon Bomb with B-29 aircraft. (*Photo: United States Air Force*)

hexagonal tail shroud which housed a flare and the control surfaces. These were operated by a controller in the launch aircraft, who kept the tail flare of the weapon in sight and operated the controls of the bomb by radio to guide the weapon on to its target.

The Tarzon entered service too late for the Second World War. Interestingly enough, these weapons were later used in the Korean war where, in 1951, three specially modified B-29s of the 19th Bombardment Group employed them in successful attacks on targets such as the Hwach-On reservoir, the Kanggye railway bridge (13 January) and the Koindong railway bridge. All told, 30 Tarzons were dropped during the campaign. Between them, they destroyed six bridges and damaged one more; three of the weapons failed, and 19 missed their target. Although moderately successful, the Tarzon was found to have one very serious operating problem in that it could not be safe-salvoed, a procedure often essential in order to jettison the weapon from an aircraft that had sustained battle or other damage. The otherwise inexplicable loss of at least one B-29 was ascribed to this failing, and Tarzon was withdrawn from service in August 1951.

Another and even more unconventional American weapon that was employed operationally during the Second World War was quite literally an unmanned aircraft. Under code-name Aphrodite, time-expired B-17s were stripped of all unneeded equipment, fitted with radio-control mechanisms and had the top deck rebuilt to include an open cockpit, (Figure 3.12). They were then loaded with 20,000lb. of explosive, usually Torpex, and used as flying bombs. The control aircraft employed were ex-RAF B-35 Venturas, and what today would be called an attack-package of

FIG. 3.12. BQ-7 Aphrodite Pilotless B-17 aircraft. (*Photos: Smithsonian Institute*)

aircraft was completed by another B-17 to act as navigation leader, a fighter escort and, finally, a P-38 that was detailed off to shoot down the unmanned B-17 if it went out of control! These Aphrodite drones, operated by the 388th Bombardment Group at Knettishall, Norfolk, were crewed by a pilot and a technician whose task it was to set the radio control equipment in flight, prime the fuse and then join the pilot in baling out before the aircraft crossed the English coast on its flight to the target on the continent.

The first raid using Aphrodite aircraft was made on 4 August 1944, but with disappointing results. One machine crashed with the pilot still aboard, another was lost to the German defences and two reached the general area of their intended targets, the V-weapon sites at Minnoyecques, Siracourt, Watten and Wizernes, but caused little damage. On 6 August, two more Aphrodite aircraft were directed against Watten, but one crashed on English soil and the other in the North Sea. Then on 12 August, the United States Navy joined the unmanned aircraft programme when it attempted to fly a radio-controlled explosive-laden PB4Y Liberator with Lieutenant Kennedy, the brother of the future President of the United States, as launching pilot in an attack against Heligoland. But at 15,000 feet over the Blyth estuary the aircraft blew up, scattering wreckage across a wide area and causing blast damage on the ground over an area of 6 miles. A second attempt on the same day resulted in the Liberator exploding on the German island of Heligoland, but not on its intended military target.

Meanwhile, efforts were made to improve the effectiveness of the B-17 Aphrodite by fitting a TV monitor to transmit to the control aircraft a view forward from the B-17 as well as a readout of the altimeter. With this new refinement another attack was made on 11 September, but the Aphrodite was lost to German flak as it approached the target area. On 14 September a further attempt resulted in one loss and one near miss, while four more flights during October produced one impact a quarter of a mile from the target, one aircraft lost to flak and two more that disappeared apparently out of control, one over the North Sea and one over the Continent. Final efforts to refine the weapon further now included remotely-controlled throttles, so that Aphrodite could fly most of the one-way mission at medium altitude, but then, using the TV monitored altimeter and the throttles, the controller would be able to bring the machine down to as low as 300 feet for the final approach to the target area in an effort to evade the terminal defences.

December 1944 saw two attacks using the modified B-17s, but one aircraft was lost to flak and a second iced-up and crashed. The last missions were flown on 1 January 1945 when two aircraft impacted well outside the target area. Before any further attempts could be made, the Aphrodite venture was cancelled. It had proved to be a very inaccurate weapon, and one that was vulnerable both to German defences and to adverse weather conditions. In any case the need for an unmanned attack weapon at this stage of the war was less than pressing, and no further American projects of this kind were attempted. The significance of the Aphrodite programme was that these aircraft seem to have been the first hesitant operational efforts in the development of guided weapons by the United States.

GERMAN AND ALLIED IMPERATIVES

As in the case of the innovations introduced by the Germans, it is clear that there were interesting, if less significant, attempts by the Allies, and particularly by the United States, to employ unmanned systems of various kinds. The circumstances were, however, far less pressing for the Allies than for the Germans. And although it is true that very heavy United States Army Air Corps losses in daylight raids over Germany in 1944 had led to the tentative use of stand-off weapons, two factors distinguished those attacks from the kind of missions flown by the Luftwaffe against, for example, the Italian Fleet or the Salerno and Anzio landing operations. First, with the exception of attacks on difficult targets such as bridges, the American raids were most commonly made against large area targets rather than point targets such as warships. Second, at the stage of the war that saw the introduction of such American weapons as the GB-1, answers, notably in the field of electronic warfare, were being found to counter enemy radar-directed guns. In any case, the war was over before the early, crude guided bombs could be perfected.

As to true unmanned aircraft, again the imperatives were of quite different orders. The German V1 campaign was explicitly designed to make effective use of available resources and to avoid putting valuable aircrews at risk, an ambition that was not, of course, fully realised in the costly offensive employing air-launched V1s. Much the same can be said of the abortive German attempts to produce operational anti-air-craft rockets. In short, because of wider constraints on resources and on trained manpower, the Germans chose the only real options still open to them. In the case of the Americans, however, the provision of material resources was never in real doubt and the sheer weight of their military effort was enough to ensure eventual supremacy in what had become a campaign of attrition. The use of Aphrodite B-17s was simply an expedient, a convenient—though inefficient—and as it turned out, dangerous, method of employing time-expired aircraft. There was never any real Allied need for surface-to-air missiles, and there was never any suggestion that aircraft other than tired veterans should be used in the terminal fashion of the Aphrodite venture. Nor does there seem to have been much interest in other unmanned attack aircraft, although both the Army Air Corps and the US Navy were, as we shall see, experimenting with a whole range of unmanned aircraft for a variety of roles.

4

The Missile Age

EARLY AMERICAN SYSTEMS

As we have seen, both the United States Navy and Army Air Corps had long shown an interest in drones for operational missions. In the US Navy, tentative experiments with target drones had been carried out in the mid-1920s and again in the mid-1930s. By 1938, radio drones had been employed as targets by the aircraft carrier USS *Ranger*, and the promising results of this venture led to proposals for an operational role for these vehicles and as for similar unmanned aircraft. Experiments using target drones to simulate attack followed in September 1940 and, as early as August 1941, an American drone was tested carrying TV to extend the visual range of the drone operator.

The encouraging progress that was then made led to a decision in November 1941 to convert 100 obsolescent torpedo bombers into attack drones, a step that was hastily reversed following the attack on Pearl Harbor, although a programme for the procurement of 100 specially designed attack drones was allowed to continue. In April 1942, the United States Navy carried out experiments with drones that marked important advances in the operational potential of these weapons. In one demonstration, a TG-2 torpedo-carrying drone was launched from its parent ship and, monitored by a TV link in an escort aircraft, detected at a range of eight miles its target destroyer, towards which it was then directed by a radio-link. At 300 yards range, the torpedo was released and travelled directly below the target's hull, as intended. In a second experiment, a BG-1 drone detected a target being towed along at a speed of eight knots at a range of four miles. By means of a TV link and radio control from a parent aircraft at a range of 30 miles, the drone was flown down on to the target and scored a direct hit.

In the light of this kind of successful experiment, the United States Naval Staff pressed for an expanded programme of drones, but three arguments now emerged. Admiral King, the professional head of the United States Navy, was anxious not to commit the new weapons to combat in the piecemeal fashion that had characterised and diminished the impact of weapons such as tanks during the First World War. Admiral Towers, on the other hand, as head of United States Naval Aviation, was opposed to any programme of production until the new device had shown itself to be superior in combat to the conventional manned aircraft of the fleet. The third argument arose from the practical question of resources. The proposal to build a force of 1,000 drones was found to imply a commitment of 10,000 personnel, 1,300 of whom would be aircrew, and it entailed a cost of $235 million. At a time when resources of all kinds were being pressed into the expansion of conventional forces, this was an unwelcome burden. There were also several other discouraging factors.

First, so as not to deflect aircraft manufacturers from their vital task of producing conventional combat aircraft, the order for the initial batches of drones had been placed with a manufacturer unfamiliar with aeronautical construction. This led to production delays, and these were made worse by various technical problems. Second, the drones turned out to be difficult to maintain once away from the benign environment of test ranges. And third, by the time the early difficulties with the drone were being rectified, the tide of battle—particularly in the Pacific—had turned, so that Admiral Nimitz, the Commander in Chief of the United States Pacific Fleet, was reluctant to accept a new and untried weapon when the combat resources already available to him were performing so well.

The size of the drone procurement programme thus fluctuated until March 1944, when it was finally settled at 388, made up of 100 already accepted, and a total of 288 of three different types still to be delivered. Later that same year, drones were at last tested in action, though not against the main strength of the Japanese fleet. Of 46 attack drones launched at enemy targets, nine suffered mechanical failures, TV malfunctions accounted for five, Japanese defences shot down three and 29 reached their intended target.

These results were less than impressive but, in any case, the need for new weapons had receded. If the attack drones had been operationally effective in the early days of the war, there would have been more enthusiasm for them. But by the time their limited potential was realised, they had become an expensive and an unnecessary diversion of resources. In September 1944, Admiral King therefore cancelled the whole naval drone programme and offered the equipment and the associated personnel to the United States Army Air Corps, an offer which General Arnold, its head, declined.

These tentative steps forward by the United States Navy in the field of unmanned aircraft were paralleled by similar hesitant experiments by the Army Air Corps. In August 1938, the head of the Corps, then Major General Westover, had outlined a need for a low-cost aerial torpedo with a range of up to 30 miles able to put a 200–300lb warhead into an area target of two square miles. The requirement was endorsed by the new Chief of the Army Air Corps, General Arnold, in September 1939, but no manufacturer could be found to meet the specification and the proposal was dropped.

In January 1940, a new specification, this time for a 'flying bomb' with a maximum range of 100 miles and an accuracy of half a mile, was drawn up. Following proposals by General Motors, in February 1941 the Army ordered ten radio-controlled flying bombs, and in July 1942 a further five. This machine was the GM A-1, a propellor-driven high-wing monoplane designed to carry a 500lb warhead 400 miles at an airspeed of 200 mph. It proved to be a considerable disappointment.

In the flight tests held at the end of 1941, at what is now Edwards Air Force Base, the first machine crashed on take-off, and the next three, though airborne in one case for as much as one and a half hours, exhibited unsatisfactory control characteristics. Later tests with modified batches of A-1s showed little improvement, and in October 1943 the project was cancelled.

Meanwhile, in March 1942, two other United States Army unmanned aircraft projects had been initiated, one involving an aerial torpedo carrying a 2,000lb warhead, and a second with a warhead of 4,000lb. The first torpedo, the XBQ-1, crashed on its first flight and the project was cancelled. Tests with the larger weapon continued in 1943 and 1944, some of them involving a version adapted from the abortive United States Navy's programme.

The year 1943 also saw the Navy experimenting with a guided missile project, codenamed Gorgon. There were several versions of the basic design, some propelled by rockets and some by pulse-jets, with emphasis being given to the ship-to-shore attack role. Launched by catapult, Gorgon was a ship-to-shore weapon weighing almost 2,000lb. It flew at a speed of between 400 and 450 mph and was guided by radio over its maximum range of 90 miles. But the first successful flight was not made until as late as 1946, and none of these early weapons, neither the later version of the XBQ-1 nor the Gorgon project, reached anything like operational status before the end of the Second World War.

But, before the end of that war, American interest in unmanned aircraft was to be unexpectedly rekindled by the successful German V1 flying bomb. In July 1944, salvaged components from examples of that weapon, including the cheap and efficient pulse-jet engine, were taken to Wright-Patterson Field for evaluation and to be used as patterns for the construction of a version for the Army Air Corps. Three weeks later the first American flying bomb, the JB-2, was ready for trials, (JB-1 had been an abortive attempt by the Northrop Corporation to build a different missile around the pulse jet of the JB-2).

Not surprisingly, the resulting unmanned aircraft was very similar to the original V1, though slightly heavier. It was powered by a PJ-31-1 pulse-jet engine that gave it uprated thrust. The American version also differed from the German original in other respects, most significantly in the guidance system employed. Whereas the V1 had used pre-set controls, the JB-2 carried radio control and was thus a true RPV rather than a drone. The JB-2 was also equipped with a radar beacon to identify its position to a ground radar station, making remote control possible up to a range of about 100 miles. Tests showed that the accuracy was improved by these means from an error of eight miles over a firing distance of 127 miles—close to the accuracy of the V-1—down to a quarter of a mile at 100 miles range for the later versions of the JB-2.

Despite early failures in the test programme, there was considerable enthusiasm among many airmen for the new weapon, including General Arnold himself who, by January 1945 was pressing for an order of 75,000 flying bombs with the intention of being able to launch 100 a day by September of that year and to increase the firing rate several-fold in subsequent months. Other Service airmen, however, including General Spatz, the Commander of the United States Army Air Corps in Europe, were less convinced of the value of what was generally conceded to be an inaccurate weapon. It was true that it could, for example, be used as a means to harrass the enemy, particularly in periods of bad weather during which the Allied bomber forces were unable to bring to bear the full weight of their potential, but there was concern that the adoption of the new weapon might lead to an intolerable diversion of personnel; and worse, that the programme would absorb such industrial resources that the supply of conventional weapons, such as bombs or shells, would be inhibited. When closer examination of the available production facilities showed that this would indeed be the consequence of any attempt at mass production, a less ambitious programme was recommended. This would have resulted in the construction of 1,000 JB-2s from November 1945 onwards with a total order of 10,000. The end of the

Second World War, however, meant that this programme, too, was aborted, although meanwhile nearly 1,400 of the American flying bombs had been manufactured and delivered.

POST-WAR PROGRAMMES

The interest by the United States Army Air Corps in the V1 led also to experiments by the United States Navy, who wished to experiment with JB-2s launched from submarines, escort carriers and LSTs (Landing Ships Tank). A number of JB-2s were acquired by the Navy and designated the 'Loon'. However, it was not until January 1946 that the United States Navy carried out the first trial. That event turned into a failure when the engine cut and the flying bomb glided into the sea.

Despite this less than encouraging start, proposals were considered to convert an Essex class aircraft carrier and a battle cruiser to the role of Loon platform; though, in the event, the only tangible result of the whole programme was the conversion of the Submarine USS *Cusk* in early 1947. The first four launches of Loon from this boat were failures, but the fifth attempt was at last successful. Other trials then followed, but by now several competing ventures were holding out the promise of more advanced performance and in March 1950 Loon was cancelled in favour of the Regulus cruise missile, which will be described later.

Snark

Meanwhile the post-war interest of the Army Air Corps in the future of cruise missiles was confirmed when it drew up a requirement in August 1945 for a weapon capable of delivering a 2,000lb warhead over a range of up to 5,000 miles. Later, an increased payload requirement of 5,000lb was substituted, and by now Northrop was presenting proposed solutions. The specification for what became the Snark (Figure 4.1) was, however, a demanding one, and this, together with budgetary difficulties that led at one stage to the cancellation of the project, meant that the first, and unsuccessful launch was not made until December 1950. That failure was to be only the first setback in the long saga that preceded the entry of Snark into operational service.

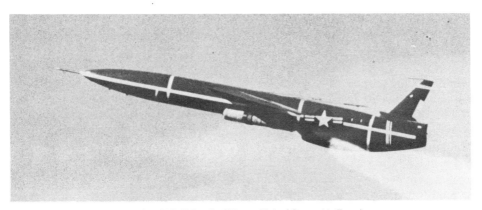

Fig. 4.1. SM-62 Snark. (*Photo: United States Air Force*)

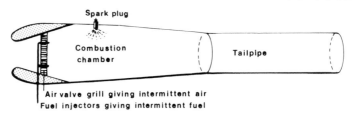

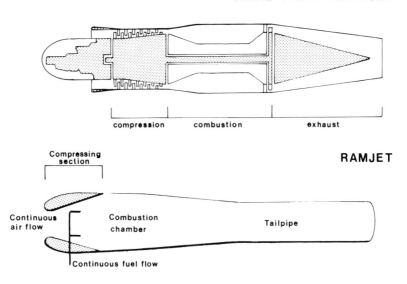

Fig. 4.2. Propulsion for Cruise Missiles.

The original version of Snark was designated by Northrop the N25. This was a 60 foot long, 28,000lb missile with a wingspan of over 42 feet. It was designed to be launched by two solid-propellant booster rockets and to be sustained in flight by a J-33 turbo-jet engine. Turbo-jet engines, (Figure 4.2) as used in Snark and in many later cruise missiles, are in effect small versions of the type of engine used in conventional jet aircraft. They are very efficient over the kind of ranges needed by cruise missiles, particularly once they have accelerated to cruising speed—hence the use of booster-rockets. Turbo-jets take ambient air at the inlet end of the engine, and compress it by means of a turbine before distributing it to combustion chambers. The resulting exhaust both provides thrust, and drives the front-end turbine by means of another turbine mounted in the path of the exhaust jet.

For the Snark trials in 1951, the 16 missiles in the programme flew a total of 21 sorties. Guided by an accompanying B-45 control aircraft, the N25 eventually demonstrated a top speed of Mach .9 and a maximum endurance of 2 hours 46 minutes. Ten missiles survived the programme; the other eleven crashed or exploded for a variety of different technical reasons. Apart from the obvious question of overall system reliability, the main problem facing the designers of the Snark was that of providing acceptable accuracy over the specified intercontinental range of the weapon. The solution offered by Northrop was an inertial navigation system monitored and updated by stellar navigation.

This stellar-inertial guidance system had three main components. First, an inertial platform which, over short distances and limited time-spans, provided the necessary data for navigation. With the gyroscopes available at the end of the 1950s, the random drift in an inertial platform could be expected to introduce an error of perhaps half-a-mile after 45 minutes of flight. Over the longer distances and flight times for which the Snark was designed, stellar observations then provided the corrections required to take out these errors. Second, there was a star tracking telescope using photosensitive elements to convert any relative error between the expected and the actual position of a predetermined star to electrical signals. These currents were then used to update the inertial platform and to command corrections to bring the missile back on track. Thus the inertial platform provided the stable base from which accurate sightings were made on celestial bodies, and the sightings themselves maintained the accuracy of the platform and its data by means of the third component, a computer.

Two basic types of stellar inertial systems were developed; one was the Automatic Celestial Navigation (ACN) system, in which a multiple sextant array was used to give fixes on two stars simultaneously, thus improving accuracy. One important disadvantage, however, was the need for a window large enough to view a wider area of the sky, which added to the cost because of the extremely high optical qualities required in the window. It also caused problems with light refraction induced by shock waves in the airflow over the window at high subsonic and supersonic speeds. The other system devised at this time was the Stellar Supervised Inertial Autonavigator (SSIA) system in which periodic sightings were made automatically by a single sextant. It was this SSIA system that was employed in the Snark cruise missile. Although the Northrop Company claimed an CEP accuracy of 1.4 nautical miles for the stellar-inertial guidance system, extensive tests carried out on board conventional aircraft showed it to be less than reliable over anything but short ranges; and the weight penalty of the installation, nearly one ton, also caused its value to be doubted.

These problems with Snark were bad enough but then, in mid-1950, the United States Air Force raised the operational requirement for the missile to include a payload of 5,000lb. At the same time the accuracy was to be increased to a CEP of 500 yards, (relaxed to 8,000 feet in 1954 when it was clear that new hydrogen bombs would be far more powerful than the original atomic weapons), and the missile was now also required to fly a supersonic dash at the end of the mission profile so that it would be able to outrun opposing interceptor fighters in the area of the target.

It was clear that Snark was having great difficulty in meeting even the original requirement, and since these new demands were clearly well beyond the potential of the system, it was now re-designed. The result was the N-69 version of the Snark. The wingspan of the N-69 was little changed from the original version of the missile, but the wing area was expanded by some 16 per cent by increasing the chord, and the fuselage of the new weapon was considerably longer than the original, 70 feet as against 52 feet; in other words in was almost exactly the same length as a Lancaster Mk III of the Second World War. It was thus a very large missile indeed, and its weight was now up by 77 per cent to 49,000lb with a new payload of 6,230lb. At first a J 71 turbo-jet engine was employed for the new version of the Snark, but this was later replaced by a J 57 turbo-jet which gave a thrust of 10,500lb. This propulsion was augmented for take-off by twin solid-fuel boosters each giving 105,000lb of extra thrust for four seconds, and four seconds of boost at 130,000lb thrust in the later models.

Tests showed, however, that this new version of the Snark also had serious deficiencies. The first five launches were failures for various reasons, including two occasions when the mainplanes became detached. The first successful recovery of an intact missile was not made until the thirty-first flight, on 2 October 1956, exactly three years after the planned in-service date of October 1953. Even at this stage of the programme, new difficulties still arose. Northrop had planned that the flight profile of the operational missile would include a terminal dive of the weapon on to its target, but it was found that the elevators were inadequate to induce the required pitch-down. A new concept was therefore introduced by which, at the end of its flight, the missile would describe a zero-g parabola flight path, ejecting the warhead which would then fall in a ballistic trajectory on to the target. The first missile with this new feature, the N-69C Modified, flew on 26 September 1955. By now, not unnaturally, the long delays in the programme, the inevitable rising costs and the continuing technical problems, were attracting considerable criticism. Then, after all the failures that had so far occurred at the launch of test missiles, one Snark in December 1956 exhibited a quite different pattern of failure as it flew on out of control from Cape Canaveral and headed for Brazil. It was found in the jungle by a no doubt bemused farmer in 1982.

Expensive though the missile was by now, supporters of the Snark programme were able to point out that the weapon still cost only about one twentieth the price of a B-52 bomber, and although it was, of course, a one-time system rather than a reusable aircraft, it did not put a crew at risk and overall it was claimed to be cost-effective. This argument, by now a familiar one, prevailed against the growing criticism as to the vulnerability of Snark both on the ground and in the air, and against increasing concern about its complex and unreliable navigation system. This last weakness of the Snark had never been resolved. In tests over a range of 2,000 miles, the missile produced an average CEP of 20 miles, and it was February 1960 before the Snark guidance system demonstrated anything like a satisfactory performance. Even at the end of the whole lengthy test programme the missile offered a less than 50 per cent chance of performing to the required parameters. Only one in three missiles actually left the ground at launch, and only one missile in the final ten launches of the test programme flew the intended distance to the target.

With this unhappy history behind it, Snark entered service with the 702nd Strategic Missile Wing of the United States Air Force at Presque Isle in May 1957; but by November of that year Strategic Air Command was already recommending that Snark be withdrawn. Shortly after President Kennedy came to office in 1961 he invited Congress to cancel the project (together with the Titan ICBM and several other major programmes). 702 Wing was therefore deactivated on 25 June 1961 after Snark had served for only four years in the inventory of the United States Air Force.

Navaho

Another, and even more ambitious attempt to develop a cruise missile during the early post-war years, was the Navaho programme. The origins of this weapon lay in a proposal at the end of 1945 by North American Corporation to construct an intercontinental missile based on the wartime German V2. The suggestion was that a version of the V2 should be fitted with mainplanes; then a further version would be designed to take an airbreathing turbo-jet engine in place of the rocket; and in the final stage of the development programme a powerful booster rocket would be added to give the system intercontinental range. The United States Air Force accepted the first stage of the proposal in April 1946. By March 1948, the programme had advanced to include three revised test vehicles, one with a range of 1,000 miles, a second with 3,000 miles and finally an operational missile with a range of 5,000 miles.

The first test vehicle was the X-10, a huge 70 foot long RPV powered by two turbo-jet engines, boosted by a rocket motor and fitted with a 28 foot span delta-shaped wing. It first flew in October 1953. During tests, it reached a record maximum speed of Mach 2.05. The second stage of the Navaho programme was the XSM-64, an even larger missile than the X-10 with a length of 87 feet 4 inches—about the same as a British Avro Shackleton aircraft—and having a wingspan across the diamond-shaped mainplane of 40 feet 3 inches—similar to that of wartime fighters like the Hurricane or the Typhoon. Its all-up weight was a remarkable 290,000lb, or about double that of airliners of the time such as the Stratocruiser. The missile was to be boosted by rocket and powered in its cruise mode by two Curtiss-Wright J-47 ramjets, giving a total thrust of 40,140lb.

It is pertinent to point out here that ramjets, (Figure 4.2) differ in operation both from pulse-jets, as used in the V1, and from turbo-jets, such as that employed in the Snark. A ramjet engine takes in air through a choke or diffuser in the inlet, which slows down the airflow and increases its pressure. The air is then mixed with fuel and continuously ignited by means of a spark-plug. The resulting combustion produces a jet of hot gases in the tail-pipe which react against the enclosed forward parts of the engine to generate a steady thrust. In order to produce the initial ram-air effect at the inlet, the motor must be accelerated to something approaching its cruising speed, hence the need for a booster rocket in the Navaho system. The huge size of the booster—it weighed 169,500lb—was partly explained by the fact that the XSM-64 cruise missile was launched vertically, and thus had to overcome the effects of gravity as well as accelerating to ram-jet operating speed. An extra 415,000lb of thrust for a period of 110 seconds was produced by the booster jets for this purpose. The intended range of the system, after the booster was jettisoned, was 5,500 miles in a flight path that would take it up to a cruise altitude of 45,000 feet at a maximum cruise speed of Mach 3.25.

But serious problems crippled the programme from the start. The first attempted flight in November 1956 ended in failure shortly after launch, and ten more failures on the ramp then followed before the missile even got airborne again, which it did in

March 1957, though for a flight of only a few minutes. Further failures followed and these disappointing results, coupled with concern about rising costs—combined with the recognition, as early as February 1954, that operational nuclear-tipped ICBMs were after all feasible, led to the cancellation of the Navaho programme in July 1957.

Some benefits did, however, flow from Navaho. The technical demands that the missile put on the designers in North American industries led for example to the development of new materials to withstand the extreme aerodynamic heating experienced, which could reach as much as 660 degrees at Mach 3. The advanced specification also led to the use of titanium alloys which gave a greater strength than aluminium, yet was 40 per cent lighter than steel and thus saved a great deal of weight. Other developments, such as those in propellants and in engine technology, became invaluable components in the Thor, Atlas and other ICBMs that now followed, while the Hounddog missile, the United States Navy A3-J Vigilante bomber and the nuclear submarine *Nautilus*, all benefited from the inertial guidance system that had been originally developed for Navaho.

5

More Second Generation Cruise Missiles

MATADOR AND MACE

Apart from Snark and Navaho, there was one other early post-war unmanned aircraft that seemed to hold considerable promise as an interim weapon system pending the introduction of operational ICBMs, and that was the Martin Matador (Figure 5.1). The programme began in August 1945 with a United States Army Air Force requirement for two versions of a 500 mile range surface-to-surface attack cruise missile, one version to be subsonic the other to be supersonic. The supersonic version was cancelled at a very early stage of the programme, but the proposal for a subsonic weapon survived various recommendations for its deletion, recommendations that were made largely on the grounds of cost at a time when the Defence budget was under considerable pressure. Thus Matador continued and eventually emerged to be given high priority in September 1950 during the rearmament programme of the Korean War.

The Matador tactical cruise missile was smaller than Snark, with a length of 39 feet 8 inches, and a span of 28 feet 7 inches, in other words, about the size of a contemporary fighter bomber aircraft such as the United States Navy A4D Skyhawk. The missile carried a 3,000lb warhead and it was launched from a mobile truck or trailer-mounted zero-length rail by means of a solid-fuel booster providing 57,000lb of thrust for 2.4 seconds. This gave Matador an initial velocity of 200 mph, and the J-33 turbo-jet, with its thrust of 4,600lb, then sustained the 12,000lb missile in flight at a speed of up to 650 mph over a maximum range of 620 miles.

Once again, technical problems arose. Apart from structural problems in the mainplane and tail assembly, Matador suffered from the serious limitation that affected all early post-war cruise missiles, that of a serious lack of accurate guidance over the full operational range. In the particular case of Matador, the guidance system chosen called for a ground-based operator to monitor and to control the flight-path of the missile by radio, which meant that control was limited to a line-of-sight range of less than about 250 miles.

A guidance system, known as Shanicle, was therefore added to the missile in 1954. This was a hyperbolic grid navigation system, on the same lines as that used in LORAN and DECCA systems. Navigation by means of a hyperbolic grid is achieved by using two ground radio transmitting stations, a master and a slave, situated a known distance apart (usually several hundred miles) and transmitting simultaneous radio pulses, that from the slave being triggered by the master. Because radio pulses travel at a known speed of about 0.186 miles per microsecond, the very small

43

Fig. 5.1. Martin B-61 Matador take-off. (*Photo: Glen L Martin Co, Maryland, USA*)

differences in time between the reception of the pulse from the master station and
that from the slave, can be used to measure the distance from each station. A line
joining all the points at which the signals from the two stations are simultaneously
received will be a straight line. All other points at which the same time difference in
reception is experienced, when joined together form hyperbolic curves. Another
family of hyperbolic curves is produced if a second slave station is employed. This
extension of the hyperbolic grid system, though requiring another deployed ground

or sea station, improves accuracy, and, by adding what can be seen as a degree of redundancy, can make the whole system somewhat more robust. Shanicle used a master and two slave stations in this way.

Because the heading of a cruise missile is usually accurately pre-set, the point at which the resulting track crosses given hyperbolic curves provides a fix of the position of the missile at any one time. Matadors using this kind of system were programmed to cross pre-determined hyperbolic lines at given times, and any deviation showed up as an error which the automatic guidance system fed to the controls as a command to change course.

Hyperbolic grid navigation systems are limited in range, depending on the radio frequencies employed, but no frequency will give high accuracy at the extreme ranges likely to be demanded by cruise missiles in the strategic role. Nevertheless, Shanicle did offer some improvement in accuracy over previous control systems. Skilled operators were able to demonstrate a CEP of about 500 yards by early 1960, while at the same time the United States Air Force established a 71 per cent reliability for the system as a whole.

In order to overcome the continuing range limitation of Matador, and also to eliminate the risk that the hyperbolic grid system might be jammed by hostile ECM measures, a third guidance system was now added to the missile, the Goodyear Company's ATRAN (Automatic Terrain Recognition and Navigation). This was a device that foreshadowed the terrain matching systems of the much later Tomahawk and AGM-86 cruise missiles of the mid-1970s, because, instead of relying upon distant radar monitoring and radio control, or upon artificial navigation features such as those generated by radio hyperbolic grids, the missile was designed to map-read its own way automatically to the target by radar map-reading.

In radar map-matching, a comparison is made between a radar map of the terrain to be traversed by the missile, and the actual terrain as perceived by a plan position indicator (PPI) or radar screen on board the missile. The comparison is made by rotating the PPI image over a pre-recorded negative radar picture of the terrain. When the two images precisely match, light is prevented from reaching a photo-electric tube which is connected to the controls through a complex of commutator and servo mechanisms. If, however, the two images do not match, then the electrical output of the photo-electric tube is converted into signals, through an amplifier and a commutator; these feed servo-mechanisms that re-align the two images and pass command information to the controls, thus changing the heading of the missile, or speeding up the radar film, so as to give corrections in the fore and aft sense.

One problem with such a system is that the dimension of ground features being scanned by the on-board radar appear to change in size with variations in altitude, though this can be overcome by using radar altimeters. A second difficulty with ATRAN was that radar maps of likely target countries such as the Soviet Union and China, did not exist at the time of the development of Matador, and nor in those pre-satellite days could they be obtained. Radar maps thus had to be drawn up from topographical and other information, which was not always geographically accurate and could also be badly out of date. A third problem was that the system could not be used over water or over stretches of land that were without distinguishing features—a characteristic of much of the Soviet Union.

Rather than simply add ATRAN to the existing Matador in order to overcome the difficulties that were being experienced with the guidance system of that missile, it was decided, in mid-1954, to update the basic Matador unmanned aircraft as well. This variant, the TM-61B, became known as Mace.

With a length of nearly 47 feet and a span of over 28 feet, Mace was 7 feet longer than Matador, but it retained approximately the same wingspan as the original missile. It was, however, more than 7,000lb heavier at launch, a penalty that was redressed by raising the thrust of the J-33 engine from 4,600lb to 5,200lb and by providing a 97,000lb solid-fuel booster motor to accelerate the system to its cruising speed of up to Mach .85. The result was a missile with a range of 540 miles at low level (as against Matador's 620 miles), but it was also capable of nearly 1,300 miles at high altitude. The payload remained at 3,000lb.

This ambitious system first flew in 1956, but the problems with the missile were, first, that at a unit cost of about $250,000, TM 76A (as it was now designated) was over four times as expensive as the TM-61C Matador equipped with the Shanicle navigation system. Second, there were considerable difficulties with production schedules and the engine. But third, and even worse, there were still problems with the guidance of the missile. The basic difficulty was that although Mace with ATRAN could not be jammed, and although the system was not limited to line-of-sight range, there was the problem of accurate radar maps of the terrain en-route to the potential targets. Eventually, radar maps were produced from the available and often unreliable topographical maps that did exist, but the disappointing fact was that ATRAN did not perform nearly as well as had been hoped, nor as well as was actually required for an operational system.

Recourse had meanwhile been made to an inertial navigation system, known as the AC Spark Plug Achiever, in a version of Mace designated TM-76B. This missile at last became operational in Germany in 1955 with the 38th Tactical Missile Wing, and was known as Mace-B. When deployed with United States Air Force tactical missile wings it was housed in hardened shelters, but it could also be mounted on cross-country mobile launch vehicles. Mace-B was in service for longer than Snark, but only by six years and after being deployed for a decade, the missile was withdrawn during 1968 and 1969 to be replaced by ballistic missiles.

MORE UNITED STATES NAVY SYSTEMS—REGULUS

During these same post-war years of United States Air Force trial and error, the interest of the United States Navy in cruise missiles had continued. In fact, a whole series of projects had begun as early as July 1943 with the Gorgon family of missiles already mentioned, versions of which were variously designed to be powered by rockets, pulse-jets, turbo-jets or ramjets.

The stimulus in the United States Navy for a switch from Loon and Gorgon to something more ambitious was the award, in 1947, of an Army Air Corps contract to Martin for a subsonic turbo-jet cruise missile, which later became the Matador, already described. In the atmosphere of inter-Service rivalry that existed in the United States during and after the Second World War, the Navy saw this weapon as a challenge to its own ambitions in the field of guided missiles, and therefore made proposals—also in 1947—for a similar weapon; indeed it was so similar that it incorporated the same J-33 turbo-jet engine and some of the Matador components.

Fɪɢ. 5.2. A United States Navy Regulus Cruise Missile leaves the launching pad on the fantail of the USS *Helena* (CA-74) on 6 April 1961. (*Photo: United States Navy and Military Archive Research Service* (*MARS*), Lincs)

This was the Chance-Vought Regulus (Figure 5.2). Not only was Regulus seen by the United States Navy as their entree to the field of post-war guided missiles, but it was also a step towards a vehicle that could carry atomic weapons, whose considerable weight of around 5,000 kg at this early stage in their development made them a virtually impossible weapon load for carrier-borne aircraft. Regulus I, the original version of the missile, was 32 feet long, and had a wingspan of 21 feet. Its launch weight was 14,500lb and it was accelerated to its cruise speed of 600 mph by two 33,000lb booster rockets as it left the launcher on the deck of its surfaced parent submarine to fly to a maximum range of about 600 miles.

The programme soon ran into difficulties, however, partly because at a time of defence financial retrenchment the very close similarities between Regulus and Matador raised political questions of wasteful duplication. But Regulus survived as a project because the Navy argued, first, that the system required only two ground control stations instead of the three that provided the Shanicle hyperbolic grid navigation system of the Matador; and second, that because Regulus was fitted with two integral boosters, whereas the single booster for Matador could be fitted to that missile only after it was mounted on its launch rail, the submarines that were intended to launch Matador would have to remain surfaced for a longer period, thus increasing their vulnerability to preemptive attack.

The first launch of Regulus took place in mid-1953 from the US Submarine *Tunny*, and the missile was also later fitted to aircraft carriers and to cruisers, entering operational service in 1955. Before Regulus was eventually phased out of service in 1964, it had developed into a system capable of carrying the smaller-sized nuclear weapon of 3.8 megatons yield that had by then been produced, and it could cover a range of up to 575 miles at a maximum speed of Mach .87, though it has to be said that the capability to make anything like an accurate delivery of warheads over this kind of distance still eluded the American designers.

Regulus was originally intended to be the first of a trio of United States Navy missiles, the other two being the Grumman Rigel, expected in service by 1950, and the Triton, to be in service in 1960. But delays, production difficulties, problems in testing and finally a series of flight test failures, caused Rigel to be cancelled in 1956, and the follow-on to Regulus became a new missile by Chance-Vought, designated Regulus II.

The ill-fated Regulus II was planned to enter service by 1957, and the first missile flew on trial in June 1956. Out of 48 tests that then followed, thirty were successful, fourteen were partly successful and only four were failures. Encouraged by this, a production contract was signed in January 1958. Regulus II was designed to carry a warhead of almost 3,000lb over a range of 570 nautical miles at Mach 2, or over a range of 1,150 miles at reduced speeds. The missile was a very large vehicle, with a length of 67 feet, a wing-span of 20 feet and a weight at launch of 22,564lb. Like the TM-76B version of the Mace missile, Regulus II was to rely on the AC Spark Plug Achiever inertial guidance system for the flight to its target. But by now the advantages of nuclear delivery by other means, particularly by ICBMs, had become overwhelmingly persuasive and with only 20 of the Regulus II missiles completed, the project was cancelled in December of the same year in which the contract had been awarded, 1958. The same fate met Triton, which at the time was seen as the ultimate cruise missile. Certainly it had very ambitious characteristics, including a range of 12,000 nautical miles, a speed of Mach 3.5 at 80,000 feet and an ability to deliver a 1,500lb warhead within 600 yards of the aiming point. This remarkable accuracy was intended to be achieved by radar map-matching, the technique used in the TM-76A Mace missile. But although Triton entered full-scale development in 1955 it never entered production. This project, too, was cancelled in the face of competition from the far more promising field of ICBM development.

Thus, if the German wartime V1, together with its derivatives, the United States Navy Loon and the United States Army Corps JB-2 are regarded as first generation cruise missiles, weapons such as Snark, Navaho, Matador, Mace and Regulus can be seen as a second generation. Their span of life extended only from the early 1950s to the end of the 1960s, when Mace-B was withdrawn from Service. Although these two decades of endeavour had produced ingenious solutions to some of the problems posed by the operational demands that this class of unmanned aircraft made, none of the programmes had been able to solve all the problems and efforts to develop cruise missiles for the long-range strike/attack role had lost momentum for the time being.

The fact was, however, that as in the case of all these second generation cruise missiles, the operational requirements were too far ahead of the available technology. This led to very serious programme delays, so that these weapons, instead of preceding ICBMs into service in the strategic role as intended, became contemporaneous with them. But the characteristics of the cruise missiles meant that they were no match for the emerging ICBMs. Ballistic missiles were proving to be more accurate and more reliable weapons, and above all they were invulnerable to enemy defences. Nor were the cruise missiles able to compete with the advantages of the manned bomber.

Even ignoring the emotional but natural reluctance among airmen to accept unmanned aircraft, there were familiar but nonetheless very real operational objections. First, bombs and bombers were proven weapons that could hit distant targets with very reasonable accuracy; cruise missiles on the other hand were showing themselves to be often wildly inaccurate. Second, cruise missiles were more vulnerable than the bomber to enemy defences because they not only flew a steady and thus predictable flight path, but they carried no defences, either passive or active. Third, cruise missiles lacked the flexibility of the manned bomber. They could not disperse for survival; they could not adopt an ostentatious alert posture in a crisis; they could not be recalled from missions, nor could they be diverted during flight; and they could fly only one, terminal, sortie. It was true that cruise missiles put no crews at risk, and that they were far less costly than bombers, but these advantages were not enough to prevent the demise in the late 1950s of the cruise missile in favour of the manned bomber and the ICBM.

6

Towards Third Generation Cruise Missiles

ICBMs TAKE THE LEAD

Ballistic missiles designed for the strategic role require high acceleration at launch, and thus very large quantities of fuel, in order to boost them into their required trajectory and to give them the velocity that will carry them over the long ranges for which they are intended. In a typical single-stage intercontinental ballistic missile, this large quantity of fuel can take up as much as 93 per cent of the total mass of the whole system, leaving only 7 per cent for the motor, the guidance system and the structure of the missile itself. The actual payload may be as little as 3 per cent of the whole.

Thus in the late 1940s and early 1950s when the somewhat crude early atomic warheads weighed as much as 5,000 kg, any intercontinental missile to carry them was bound to be not only an enormous and unwieldly vehicle, but its development, particularly in terms of the required accuracy, was beyond the emerging technology of the time. Hence the emphasis on cruise missiles, and the constant efforts to overcome the most serious drawback in cruise missile systems—the inaccuracy of delivery—which also affected these weapons.

Even by 1958, inertial guidance systems were still demonstrating errors of .03 degrees per hour, or almost 2 miles for a cruise missile flying for one hour at 600 knots. Most of the missiles were, of course, required to fly a great deal further than this and the resulting errors were then so gross as to be barely acceptable, even with the more powerful warheads that were by now becoming available and even against very large targets such as major conurbations. Nevertheless, cruise missiles were the only practicable alternative to the manned bomber. In consequence, intercontinental ballistic missiles were accorded a much lower priority than cruise missiles. During the years 1951 to 1954, for example, the Atlas ICBM programme attracted $26.2 million of funding, while Snark and Navaho between them claimed a total of $450 million of defence finance.

In October 1953, this perception of the relative value of the two types of missile changed sharply when it became clear that much smaller and thus much lighter nuclear warheads could be produced. A one-megaton weapon would soon be available, for example, that weighed only between 1,500 and 3,000lb.

This development meant that nuclear-tipped ballistic missiles with strategic ranges were, after all, feasible, and work on systems such as Atlas, Thor and Titan was accelerated. As a result, the first medium range ballistic missile, Thor, was eventually launched in January 1957, the first Titan followed in February 1959, and the Atlas went on to reach full operational status in October 1959, five months ahead of Snark.

In the strike role, the ballistic missile had thus overtaken the cruise missile, and indeed other factors now served to widen the gap between the two competing families of systems. First, an ICBM could reach its target in minutes as compared to the several hours likely to be needed by a cruise missile, and this much shorter flight time contributed to the greater accuracy of the ICBM, since errors in inertial guidance platforms are a function of time. And second, as has been mentioned, the steady flight path of all cruise missiles made them highly vulnerable to opposing defences, whereas there was no defence at all against ICBMs. Third, there may also have been an element of prestige in the equation; the Soviets were developing ballistic missiles, and in October 1957 they had caused profound dismay in the United States and, indeed, in much of the Western world, by launching the Sputnik I satellite by this means. The United States was bound to follow with its own accelerated ICBM programme. All these factors thus combined in the late 1950s to shift the emphasis in the United States from what had once seemed a very promising programme of cruise missiles to a programme of intercontinental ballistic missiles.

But nuclear strike was not the only role in which cruise missiles were seen to have a role. The same concern about the growing effectiveness of Soviet air defences that had led to unease about the vulnerability in flight of cruise missiles, was also leading to a search for means of improving the survivability of manned bombers. This led to the development of cruise missiles in two other important roles; as decoys, and as airborne stand-off weapons.

CRUISE MISSILES AS DECOYS

Airborne decoys are unmanned aircraft of modest size designed to simulate the characteristics of larger attack aircraft; and since radar is the principal means by which aircraft are detected, identified, acquired and engaged by opposing defences, it is on the radar characteristics or signature that most of the emphasis is placed in the design of decoy aircraft. During the mid-1950s, the United States Air Force developed three systems for this role. The first was the Consolidated-Vultee Buck Duck, which underwent trials during the early months of 1955. This decoy was designed to simulate the huge B-36 bomber, but it was so delayed in development that it would have seen only 12 months of service before the B-36 itself was replaced by the B-52. Buck Duck was therefore cancelled as a project in January 1956.

A second decoy aircraft was the Bull Goose, a Fairchild development started in 1952. Unlike the Buck Duck that was designed to be carried by attacking bombers, Bull Goose was a ground-launched device. It was a delta-winged aircraft weighing 7,700lb at launch, including a 500lb electronic countermeasure (ECM) payload. The specification called for a 4,000 km range, with an accuracy of plus or minus 100 km—perfectly adequate for a decoy rather than for a strike weapon, and it called for a speed of Mach .85 so as to reproduce the kind of performance of which contemporary bombers were capable. But trials showed that Bull Goose could not, after all, convincingly simulate the B-52 on radar and in 1957 this project too was cancelled.

Finally, there was the much more successful Quail decoy. Quail, (Figure 6.1) was developed from an operational requirement of January 1956 for an aircraft to

FIG. 6.1. GAM-72 QUAIL ECM Carrier aboard its trolley. Early 1960s. (*Photo: McDonnell Douglas Corporation and MARS*)

simulate United States Air Force bomber aircraft. In its original form (GAM-72), it was a delta-wing vehicle powered by a J85 turbo-jet and with a span of 5 feet and a length of 9 feet. It weighed just over 1,000lb, of which in the initial models 100lb was an ECM package; later versions also carried chaff and an infra-red decoy. The normal decoy load of a B-52 bomber was four Quails, and that of the B-47 two. When deployed, the decoy could operate up to an altitude of 50,000 feet at speeds as high as .9 Mach and with a range of as much as 445 nautical miles. In flight the slab-sided configuration of Quail, together with two ventral and two vertical fins, complemented by the ECM load, produced a simulated radar image of the B-52, while its aerodynamic performance was also close to that of the bomber. Among other attributes, the decoy could be programmed to make at least two changes of heading in flight and one in airspeed, thus replicating some of the other characteristics that could be expected of a manned bomber.

The first Quails were accepted into service in September 1960. By April 1962, a total of fourteen B-52 squadrons had been declared operational with this decoy device. By the end of the production run, 616 Quails had been manufactured, including a second version (GAM-72A) which carried a revised mark of the J85 engine. Unfortunately, this modified engine proved to be heavier than the original model for the same thrust of 2,450lb, and combined with smaller wing configuration, the new Quail turned out to have a reduced range and a reduced payload when flown at the same airspeed as the original version.

However, the main problem with the whole system was wider than this. First, the technical reliability of Quail proved to be disappointing. Second, in a trial held in 1972, United States Air Force radar controllers proved able to distinguish Quail from B-52 bombers in 21 runs out of 23. Third, by now the radars available to potential opponents, notably of course to the Soviet Union, had been refined to a stage well beyond that for which the Quail was designed as an effective decoy. As early as 1969, Quail was seen to be less than operationally effective and the system was therefore phased out in the late 1970s.

STAND-OFF CRUISE MISSILES

The other role foreseen for unmanned aircraft at this time was that of stand-off strike or attack weapons. There were two significant United States Air Force developments; The GAM-67 Crossbow and the AGM-28 Hounddog. Crossbow was an air-to-ground cruise missile designed to home on to enemy air defence radars. Designed by the Radiophone Company to meet an operational requirement of the early 1950s, Crossbow was a high-wing twin-fin weapon carrying a 1,000lb warhead. It was intended to be carried on Strategic Air Command bombers and to be launched outside the cover of opposing radars at an altitude of around 34,000 feet. It would then climb under its own power to 40,000 feet and fly at 480 knots until it was within a few miies of the emitting enemy radar, at which point it would dive at an angle of 30 degrees, still under power, to strike its target. Tests began in late 1955, and the first guided flight took place in May 1957. It was found, however, that not only did Crossbow have a slower airspeed than required, but its range turned out to be less than that of Soviet radars. This was critical, and, during a period of financial cutbacks, it was judged imprudent to invest further resources in efforts to improve the performance of Crossbow, with the result that the project was cancelled in June 1957.

Hounddog was the North American Aviation response to a United States Air Force requirement of 1956 for an air-to-surface missile with which to arm the B-52 bomber. The project was accelerated in February 1958 at a time when the United States Air Force was concerned both about what was seen to be an unfavourable shift in the strategic balance caused partly by Soviet successes with ballistic missiles, and about a growing effectiveness in Soviet air defences. A stand-off weapon would enable a B-52 to remain outside the worst of the Soviet defensive array, yet still deliver a very heavy nuclear strike.

Hounddog was a 5-ton 42 foot long missile powered by an underslung J-52 turbo-jet engine. It had a 12 foot span delta-configured mainplane and small canard foreplanes. The warhead was a four-megaton device weighing 1,740lb, which could be carried over a maximum range of 675 miles at a top speed for the missile of Mach 2.0. The first production Hounddogs were delivered in December 1959, and by 1963 no fewer than 593 missiles were in service with the B-52, an aircraft that carried two of the weapons—one under each wing, mounted between the fuselage and the inner engine nacelles.

The Hounddog missile was a reasonably successful venture because, although its inertial navigation guidance system produced errors of about one mile over the maximum range, this was not critical with the size of nuclear warhead fitted. But less satisfactory features were, first, the general unreliability of the missile; and second, the undesirable addition to the drag of the parent bomber that the Hounddogs generated, thus reducing the top speed of the B-52 aircraft. These considerations led to Hounddog being phased out in 1976, to be replaced by the much lighter, smaller and faster SRAM (Short Range Attack Missile), of which by 1974 over 11,000 were fitted to the fleet of B-52 bombers.

SCUD, SCAM and SCAD

By this time, further concerns about likely Soviet developments in the air defence field had emphasised the parallel need for a Quail replacement. Assessments by the United States Air Force authorities forecast that these Soviet air defence develop-ments would soon include AWACS (Airborne Warning and Control Systems), as well as look-down/shoot-down interceptors, that is to say aircraft that could scan by radar below their own altitude so as to detect low-flying enemy bombers, and engage them with missiles whose effectiveness in homing on to their targets would not be reduced by radar or infra-red returns from the ground.

Studies were therefore made of the requirement and two possible successors to Quail were suggested; SCUD, (Subsonic Cruise Unarmed Decoy), an advanced decoy cruise missile with a range of 2,000 kilometres and a speed of .85 Mach; and SCAM (Subsonic Cruise Attack Missile), an armed version of the same basic vehicle. Meanwhile RAND Corporation proposed a longer-range cruise missile that could be launched from the SRAM launcher of the B-52 bomber. The B-52 SRAM launcher was a rotating weapon rack that had by now been developed to be carried in the bomb-bay. It did not merely release weapons such as SCAM, it also launched them forward with the necessary velocity to give them full self-sustaining flight.

Further studies showed that SCAM was technically feasible, that it could be adapted to fit the SRAM launcher and that it could be employed by the B-52 in three ways: as a straightforward decoy; as an armed decoy; or as an attack missile in its own right.

At the same time, the United States Air Force Air Systems Command put forward proposals for yet another cruise missile, the SCAD (Subsonic Cruise Armed Decoy), carrying an ECM package weighing 20lb, which would equip the B-52 in the decoy role. After considerable in-fighting and not a little delay, a relatively inexpensive, modular version of SCAD was finally approved in July 1970. It was to be primarily a decoy for internal carriage in the B-52. This important fact then determined the size and the general configuration of the weapon, notably it trapezoidal cross-section, which meant that a greater density of missiles could be packed into the essentially circular cross-sectional form of the SRAM launcher.

After further disputes between the Air Force, who insisted on SCAD as a penetration aid for manned bombers, and Congress who pressed for it to be developed as a stand-off weapon, contracts were let in the first half of 1972 for the decoy version of the missile. Even now, however, the matter was not settled. As development work went on, two studies in 1973 again criticised the SCAD pro-gramme. One study, carried out by the Government Accounting Office, pointed out that because of delays in the project, SCAD would not enter service until two years after the threat it was designed to counter. A second study, this time by the Air Force itself, showed that while SCAD was essential to the success of B-52 missions, it raised the survivability of the successor aircraft, the B-1 bomber, by only one per cent.

At the same time, it emerged that SCAD would not, as the Air Force had claimed, be compatible both with the B-52 and with the B-1; the airframe and the electronic package would in fact need to be quite different. This disclosure opened the whole subject once again and with further scrutiny even more serious problems emerged. First, it was late. Second, its development costs had escalated from $285 million to $605 million in only six months. Third, the Soviets had not, as forecast, deployed AWACS, nor had they fielded the expected look-down/shoot-down interceptor aircraft. Fourth, the ECM package in the decoy was not up to specification. Finally, the Air Force had wanted a simple decoy all along, while Congress was still pressing for an attack weapon. This dichotomy of views left the United States Air Force isolated in the face of mounting criticism, and the result was that in July 1973 SCAD was cancelled by the Department of Defence; the Air Force did not, after all, procure its intended replacement for the Quail decoy.

THE *EILAT* SINKING

The reluctance of the United States Air Force to re-enter the field of strike or attack cruise missiles was matched for a time by a similar lack of enthusiasm in the United States Navy for these weapons. Meanwhile, the Soviet fleet had put considerable emphasis on cruise missiles, partly no doubt to compensate for the absence of carrier-borne aviation in that navy. But the Soviets had also exported some varieties of their cruise missiles to certain of their client states and their allies, one of them being Egypt, which received among other weapon systems, the SS-N-2 Styx anti-ship cruise missile (Figure 6.2). In October 1967, one of these missiles sank the Israeli destroyer *Eilat*. As so often happens in matters of military procurement, this single, very practical, demonstration of the effectiveness of cruise missiles led to a renewed and widespread interest in the cruise missile as a weapon, not least in the United States Navy.

As luck would have it, McDonnell-Douglas had started private-venture studies into anti-shipping missiles during 1965, and when, following the *Eilat* sinking, the American Navy put out a study contract to explore the possibility of these missiles for its own purposes, the company was able to make a prompt response. This was the start of the AGM-84 Harpoon programme which had as its objective an anti-ship sea-skimming missile able to carry a 250lb conventional warhead over a range of 40 nautical miles. Tests of the missile began in 1972 and the first successful flight was made at the end of that year by a version of the weapon that carried a warhead of 500lb and gave a range of 60 kilometres. Pilot production began in the middle of 1974 and full production started in 1976. By late 1979, over 1,000 Harpoons had been delivered and, by early the next year, another 1,735 were on order. By the end of 1980, something like 100 surface ships, 29 submarines and seven squadrons of aircraft were equipped with the Harpoon missile.

Briefly, the Harpoon missile is 3.8 metres long without the booster fitted, and has a diameter of only 34 centimetres. Cruciform mainplanes with a span of 91 centimetres are fitted, and control is provided by four all-moving fins. With a booster fitted for ship-board launch the missile weighs 667 kilogrammes; without the booster, and thus for airborne launch, it weighs 522 kilogrammes.

FIG. 6.2. A SS-N-2 anti-ship cruise missile is loaded onto its launcher. Early 1960s. (*Photo: TASS. Print from MARS, Lincs*)

In operation, the Harpoon cruise missile is simply launched from aircraft, or, in the case of ship or submarine launch, it is propelled after release by a solid-fuel booster rocket until it attains cruising speed. It then descends to a height of between 50 and about 200 feet above the surface of the sea, flying at a high subsonic Mach number of 0.85. It uses a Northrop inertial guidance system and it is maintained in its sea-skimming flight profile by means of a radio altimeter. Once in range of its target, a Texas Instruments DSQ-28 active radar homing terminal guidance system locks on, and this radar can do so effectively even in bad weather and in high seas. The system also includes electronic counter counter measures (ECCM). Propulsion is effected by means of a Teledyne J402 turbo-jet engine, and the warhead is a 500lb penetration type with HE blast-effect filling. There is no nuclear version of the missile.

Four variants of the basic missile were eventually produced: AGM-84A, which is programmed for a terminal pop-up manoeuvre, designed both to defeat short-range AA defences at the target and to increase warhead penetration; AGM-84B, a missile without a pop-up manoeuvre but with good target penetration; AGM-84C, an improved version of 84A; and AGM-84D, a version currently in production which offers a longer range and selectable terminal trajectories. As well as being capable of ship-launch, the missile can be carried by several aircraft types, including the B-52G, the Intruder, P3 Orion, Nimrod and the S-3 Viking.

The long-term significance of Harpoon was that it eventually led to more advanced weapons systems, particularly in the case of the submarine-launched version of Harpoon that was added to the programme in 1971.

A second proposal envisaged a cruise missile system launched from a new class of nuclear powered submarine, each of which boats would carry twenty vertical launch tubes to take a 30 inch diameter weapon having a range of up to 500 miles. This was known as the Submarine Tactical Antiship Weapons Systems (STAWS). Third and last, there was a proposal to fit cruise missiles into ten converted Polaris ICBM submarines, with three cruise missiles in each vertical launch tube instead of one Polaris ballistic missile. Neither of these latter two proposals was adopted, and priority was eventually given by the Chief of Naval Operations to the idea of encapsulated Harpoons launched from torpedo tubes, a decision that was shortly to gain impetus from new external factors.

Thus, by the start of the 1970s, most of the short-range United States cruise missile programmes had been suspended, and only the SRAM and the Harpoon system retained any real operational significance. The reasons were various; but they included, first, the unreliability of major component systems, including engines and guidance components; second, the vulnerability of cruise missiles to enemy active and passive defences; and third, their continuing lack of accuracy.

The problems with cruise missiles were, however, not merely technical ones. None of the United States Services were anxious at this time to accept cruise missiles in roles that might erode the principal missions of those Services. Thus, the United States Air Force had resisted the idea of air-launched cruise missiles (ALCMs) that might have replaced the manned bomber. The United States Army had declined to accept the responsibility of developing ground-launched cruise missiles (GLCMs), because of the impact that this might have had on the financial provision for systems more in keeping with the traditional roles of ground forces. And the powerful aircraft carrier element of the United States Navy was antipathetic to the notion of an anti-ship cruise missile because they saw the tasks of such a missile as being more properly the province of carrier-borne aviation.

BRITISH SYSTEMS

During the early post-war years, the Royal Air Force also showed considerable interest in stand-off weapons that could be carried by the new V-bombers, the Valiant, the Victor and the Vulcan. Two systems were designed. One was the Blue Boar guided bomb, a Vickers-Armstrong private venture which carried a Smith's autopilot and a TV camera fitted in the nose by means of which a remote operator controlled the bomb on to the target. The weapon underwent successful trials in Australia during 1954, but in June of that year the project was cancelled.

Blue Boar had been only a free-fall guided bomb, and in the early 1950s a more ambitious project was started by the Weapons Research Division of Avro's in the form of an Air-to-Surface Missile. This project coincided with an Operational Requirement issued by the Air Ministry in 1954 for a powered glide bomb for the new

FIG. 6.3. Blue Steel being loaded onto a Vulcan B2 bomber. (*Photo: MOD. Crown copyright*)

V-bombers. The intention was to be able to deliver a nuclear warhead using an inertial guidance system so that the parent aircraft could release the weapon and turn away outside the most dense concentrations of enemy ground-based defences. It was this weapon that became 'Blue Steel'.

It was a large missile, carrying a megaton warhead. It had a length of 34 feet 9 inches, a diameter of 68 inches, a wingspan of 12 feet 11 inches and a launch weight of 15,000lb. The fuel for its rocket motor was Kerosene and hydrogen peroxide (the latter being a substance that greatly complicated the ground-handling of the weapon), giving a hypersonic cruise speed and a range that at first was only about 100 miles. This meant that the bomber would still need to penetrate any peripheral defences on its route to the target; but the weapon could then be released outside the more dense terminal defences of the target area thus giving the aircraft a much higher chance of survival. Blue Steel was a complex system incorporating an autopilot, an onboard computer and electrically operated flying controls. These consisted of an all-moving foreplane and inboard ailerons on the wings, and the weapon was manoeuvred on the twist-and-steer principle. The weapon was carried singly, recessed into the belly of the carrier aircraft. At the release point, the on-board computer of the missile was updated so that its precise position heading and speed is known to the computer, and after falling free for a short space of time, the missile gave the command to ignite the two-chamber motor. It was first tested in 1957, and a year later a full test-launch was made from a Valiant with a Blue Steel powered by a de Havilland Double-Spectre engine. The Mark I version of the weapon entered service with No. 617 Squadron, equipped with Vulcan B2s, in June 1962, and it later also equipped Nos. 27 and 83 Vulcan Squadrons as well as Victor B2s of Nos. 100 and 139 Squadrons. In August 1958 an initial study was started for a Mark II version of

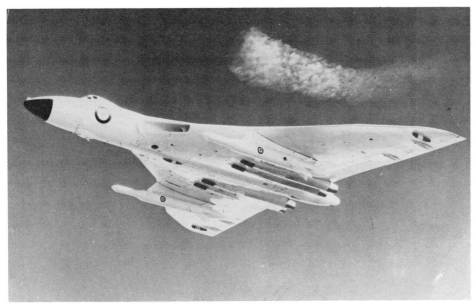

FIG. 6.4. Vulcan bomber carrying two Skybolt missiles. (*Photo: MOD. Crown copyright*)

Blue Steel powered by four ram-jet engines, but after only a limited amount of work had been completed, the project was cancelled in December 1959.

By the mid-1960s the original version of the weapon had been modified so as to improve its ability to penetrate hostile airspace, and was adapted for release at the low levels of operation that had meanwhile been introduced for the V-force, and its range was increased. But by now an agreement had been reached with the United States to purchase the ill-fated Skybolt (Figure 6.4) air-launched ballistic missile, and Blue Steel was progressively withdrawn from service.

SOVIET UNMANNED AIRCRAFT

A brief mention of Soviet unmanned aircraft must be made, though it should be stressed that the technical details of these systems are often obscure. The Soviet programme began with tests in the Baltic soon after the Second World War using captured V2s. This then led to the development of medium range ballistic missiles such as the SSN-3 and 4, and to ICBMs such as the crude SS-6 Sapwood whose 32 liquid-fuelled motors were used to launch the first Sputnik satellite in October 1957. Work on cruise missiles went on in parallel with that on ballistic systems, the first practical result of which, the air launched AS1 Kennel, (Figure 6.5) was deployed from 1957 onwards, as was the first Soviet naval cruise missile, the SSN-2 Styx.

Other cruise missiles or variants of them followed at a rate of almost one each year, as Figure 6.6 illustrates. The Soviet programme tended at first to concentrate on cruise missiles for maritime roles, and in particular on systems with which to neutralize the United States aircraft carriers, ships which at that time posed one of the principal strike threats to the Soviet homeland. In 1953 for example, the United

Fig. 6.5. AS-1 Kennel being prepared for a training shoot. (*Photo: Fotokhronike TASS*)

States Navy contained no fewer than twenty-six carriers, of which an estimated fourteen could deploy to sea at any one time to launch strike aircraft at Soviet mainland targets from the Atlantic, the Mediterranean, the Indian Ocean or from the Pacific Ocean. Believing themselves thus threatened by the United States, it was vital for the Soviets to be able to counter or to neutralise the potential of these powerful ships.

The result was that over the years the Soviet Navy deployed a whole family of surface-to-surface cruise missiles on many of its surface ships and on some classes of submarines. An improved version of the Styx (Figure 6.2) for example, was fitted to the Kildin and Kashin classes of destroyer and to the OSA 1, Matka and Tarantula classes of missile patrol boats. The Styx missile has a range of about 40 nautical miles, flies at a speed of 0.9 Mach and delivers a 1,000lb HE warhead. It has seen service in three wars: the Arab–Israeli conflict of 1967, when it was employed among other things to sink the Israeli destroyer Elat; the Indo-Pakistan war of 1971; and the Yom Kippur war of 1973. Later versions of the missile are still in service, not only with the Soviet Navy but also with the navies of Algeria, Cuba, Indonesia, Iraq, Libya, North Korea and several other nations world-wide. Later Soviet surface-to-surface missiles include the Shaddock SS-N-3, which can be launched from Echo II (Figure 6.7) and Juliet class submarines with a range of about 250 nautical miles; and the SS-N19 introduced in 1981 with a range of 250 nautical miles and deployed on Oscar class submarines as well as on the Kirov class of cruisers.

The early Kennel air-to-surface missile was followed by the AS-2 Kipper and by the AS-3 Kangaroo, a weapon first deployed on Bear B & C bombers in 1960, and

Soviet Union

Year	Designation	Silhouette	Length in feet
1956	AS-1		27.7
1956	SSC-2b		27.2
1956	SS-N-1		22.5
1959	SS-N-2a		21.5
1960	AS-2		32.9
1961	AS-3		49.1
1962	SS-N-3c		36.5
1962	SSC-1a	Not available	. . .
1965	AS-5		28.2
1965	SS-N-3a		38.5
1967	AS-4		37.1
1967	SS-N-3b		33.5
1967	SSC-1b	Not available	. . .
1968	SS-N-7		23
1970	SS-N-9		29
1970	AS-6	Not available	. . .
1974	SS-N-14	Not available	. . .
1975	SS-N-2c		21.5
1977	SS-N-12		38.5

United States

Year	Designation	Silhouette	Length
1952	Matador		39.7
1956	Regulus I		33
1958	Regulus II		57
1958	Snark		70
1958	Mace		44
1961	Hound Dog		42.5
1970	ALCM/SCAD		14
1970	Harpoon		12.6
1975	Tomahawk		20.5

Source: Based on "U.S. Cruise Missiles," Supplemental Submission by Rear Admiral Walter M. Locke, USN, Director, Joint Cruise Missiles Project, to the House Appropriations Committee. April 30, 1979.

FIG. 6.6. Progressive introduction of the Cruise Missile: United States and Soviet Union 1951–1980. (*From: Cruise Missiles Technology Strategy Politics by Richard K. Betts. Pub. Brookings Institute, Washington 1981*)

FIG. 6.7. Echo II (SSGN) with SS-N-3A launch tubes elevated. (*Photo: MOD. Crown copyright*)

FIG. 6.8. AS-3 Air-to-Surface Missile on Bear B/C. (*Photo: MOD. Crown copyright*)

FIG. 6.9. AS-4 Kitchen missile on Backfire bomber. (*Photo: Royal Swedish Air Force*)

still in service, (Figure 6.8). With a length of 49 feet, and a launch weight of 18,000lbs, the Kangaroo is a very large subsonic weapon with a range of perhaps as much as 350 nautical miles, and designed to deliver either a nuclear warhead of 800KT or a conventional load of 5,070lb. Subsequent ASMs included the AS-4 Kitchen, (Figure 6.9), the AS-5 Kelt and the AS-6 Kingfish (Figure 6.10). This latter missile is another large device having a length of 34.5 feet and a wingspan of 8 feet. Launched from Badger C and G bombers, it travels at a speed of Mach 3 over a range of 150–250 nautical miles to deliver either a nuclear warhead of 200KT or a conventional one of 2,000lb HE.

More recently the AS-15 has been added to the Soviet air-to-surface armoury. This is a cruise missile much like the United States Air Force Tomahawk GLCM. It has a range of about 3,000 kilometres, thus putting it into the ICM bracket, and it may be fitted with guidance equipment similar to the United States Tercom system, which, it is believed could give it a CEP of about 150 feet at the target. This small subsonic and low altitude Cruise Missile is at present deployed on Bear H aircraft and it is expected to be carried by Blackjack when that aircraft enters service.

There is also a Soviet sea-launched subsonic low altitude cruise missile, the SS-NX-21, which is small enough to be launched from conventional torpedo tubes in submarines, such as the reconfigured Yankee boats, and the new Akula and Sierra classes of SSNs. Initially the missile is expected to be armed with a nuclear warhead, but the accuracy of the system when fully developed may mean that it can be

FIG. 6.10. AS-6 Air-to-Surface Missile on Badger bomber (*Photo: MOD. Crown copyright*)

employed with a conventional payload against, for example, NATO airfields, C3 modules and above all against Alliance nuclear assets. A ground launched subsonic low altitude cruise missile, the SSC-X-4 is also under development.

Finally, in this very brief survey of Soviet unmanned aircraft, there is the system designated by NATO the SS-NX-24, which is expected to be flight tested from a converted specially Yankee-class Cruise Missile attack submarine (SSGN) and deployed operationally by 1988. It is also possible that a ground-launched version of this missile could later be developed.

One of the most striking features of the Soviet Surface-to-Surface and Air-to-Surface systems is that they employ various techniques for initial and for mid-course guidance. These include, for the initial and mid-course stages of the flight path, beam-riding, for example in the AS-3 Kangaroo, and inertial guidance as seen in the AS-4 Kitchen and the AS-6 Kingfish. For terminal guidance there are examples of the use of active radar, as in the warhead of the AS-4 Kitchen, the AS-5 Kelt, and the active radar believed to be fitted to the AS-6 Kingfish.

Thus the shifts both in Soviet strategic thought and in their assessment of the threat to the homeland have been accompanied by the steady development of unmanned aircraft in the form of cruise missiles which have been developed or adapted to meet those changing operational perceptions. In the case of Soviet air power in particular, cruise missiles, whether air, sea or ground launched, now form an important element both in their nuclear and in their conventional armouries.

7

Operational Experience With Unmanned Aircraft

THE ORIGIN OF AMERICAN OPERATIONAL SYSTEMS

The present programme of American operational drones had its beginning in the target drones produced soon after the Second World War. The Teledyne Ryan Q-2A Firebee, for example, was developed in the early 1950s as a tri-Service project to provide targets for missile and gunnery crews in surface-to-air and in air-to-air engagements. This was followed in 1958 by the prototype of the Q-2C, a much improved model of the Firebee with a better performance and a higher degree of reliability. Production began at the beginning of 1960. Another model, the Teledyne Ryan 124 Firebee I (BQM-34/MQM-34) first flew in the Summer of 1951. This was a turbo-jet powered device that could be controlled by UHF radio from the ground or from an aircraft. With a span of 12 feet 11 inches, a maximum weight of 2,500lb, and a length of 22 feet 11 inches, it was by no means the smallest of unmanned aircraft. Its performance was also noteworthy. Powered by a J69-T-2a turbo-jet engine, the machine was capable of a maximum speed of 600 knots and had a range of 692 miles. It could be air or ground launched and was equipped with a two-stage parachute recovery system. By January 1986, no fewer than 32,000 flights had been made by Firebee I targets alone and exercises had been conducted with virtually every surface-to-air and air-to-air weapon system in the arsenals of the United States Services, as well as those in numerous research and development programmes. But the long term significance of the Teledyne Ryan family of unmanned aircraft was their adaptability, and in particular of their operational potential.

Tentative work on operational drones in the United States had begun as early as 1959, when it was realised that the United States Air Force programme of high altitude reconnaissance flights over the Soviet Union, by then over three years old, might be halted if the Soviets succeeded in shooting down one of the U-2 aircraft that were employed on this covert work. These fears were realised on 1 May 1960 when a U-2 flown by Gary Powers was shot down by an SA-2 Surface-to-air missile near Sverdlovsk. The United States was thus faced with a gap in its surveillance capabilities that would last for eighteen months until the first surveillance satellite could be launched.

Two months after Powers was shot down, another American aircraft was lost, this time an RB-47 that was flying an Electronic Intelligence (ELINT) collection mission over the Barents Sea. This machine was brought down by Soviet interceptors causing the loss of five crewmen killed or missing and another two captured, a disaster that emphasised the importance of an interim programme by which to maintain surveil-

65

lance over key features of the Soviet Union. Just eight days later, the first contract, at the modest price of $200,000 was awarded to the Ryan Aeronautical Company for a test flight demonstration of how a target drone might be adapted for photographic reconnaissance tasks.

It is interesting to note that this early RPV was to be designed with low radar-reflectivity in mind, a very important aspect of covert flying which will be discussed more fully in Chapter 10. Experiments with scale models had shown that radar reflectivity could be reduced in a number of ways, including the introduction of a screen of mesh wire over the intakes, coating the nose-section with non-conductive paint and attaching a sheet of radar absorbent material to each side of the fuselage. These measures were successfully applied to full-scale versions of the RPV. Other studies meanwhile confirmed the practicality of adapting it to carry photographic reconnaissance cameras.

This promising start was however followed by disappointment for the designers when shortage of Pentagon funds caused all the available budgetary resources available for new reconnaissance assets to be devoted to the emerging SR-71 Mach-3 reconnaissance aircraft. Not until almost two years later, in February 1962, was approval given to proceed with the RPV programme, this time for Q2-C machines modified to enhance high survivability and configured to carry cameras.

The design criteria for what was known by the programme code-name Fire Fly, was that the new aircraft should have a range of 1,200 nautical miles, a cruising altitude above 55,000 feet and an ability to take photographs with the high resolution of only two feet from that height. Later, four of these early machines would be known as the Ryan 147A, the first of a long line of drones and RPVs (Figure 7.1) developed by that Company. Various other code names for the programme now followed, a confusion of nomenclature not helped by the fact that in the Spring of 1971 the drones also became known by the military designator AQM (air launched, drones, guided missile; while the B in a parallel BQM series indicated that the drone could be air or ground launched). The 147H for example became the AQM34N, and the low altitude 147SC became AQM-34L. The account given here uses the manufacturer's designation where at all possible. Tests with these first Ryan 147As were made in early 1962 when launches from C-130A launch aircraft proved the feasibility of the system, while at the same time practice interceptions by F-106 aircraft demonstrated the success of the measures that had been adopted to reduce radar reflectivity.

Meanwhile the Cuban crisis of 1962 was in gestation. On 14 October of that year an American reconnaissance aircraft had detected the installation of the first Soviet missiles in Cuba; and surveillance was maintained until 27 October 1962, when one of the many U-2 flights that were being made at that time was engaged by a Soviet-supplied surface-to-air missile and destroyed, killing the pilot. This event provided the stimulus for an acceleration of the 147 programme, and a contract now followed for the 147B model, the first true reconnaissance drone. It should be pointed out here that other operational drones were being developed in the United States at about this time, notably by the Boeing Company; but since the Ryan family of drones is better documented and since it saw far more extensive development and operational use, the expansion of drone capabilities will be less confusingly dealt with by confining this account to the Ryan products (Figure 7.2).

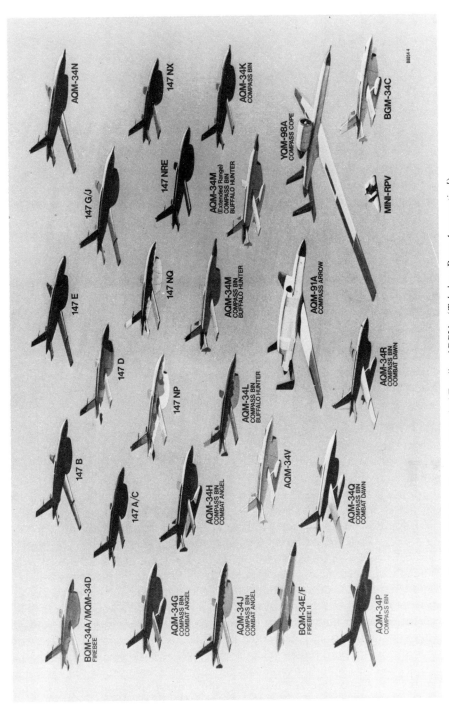

FIG. 7.1. Teledyne Ryan Aeronautical Family of RPVs. (*Teledyne Ryan Aeronautical*)

Fig. 7.2. Versions of Teledyne Ryan Aeronautical Model 147 RPVs poised in front of United States Air Force DC-130A launch aircraft with RPV loaded at wing pylon. (*Photo: Teledyne Ryan Aeronautical*)

The 147B version was an enhanced model of the original drone designed for high altitude work. Its much increased wing area gave it a ceiling of 62,500 feet, it had a range of 1,680 nautical miles and it embodied an improved navigation system using an on-board programmer and a Doppler radar. Production of seven Model Cs then followed, four of which were eventually employed operationally, three of them in Cuban ELINT collection. The other three served first in the training role and then as platforms for modifications leading to later versions of the same basic drone.

One of these versions was the 147D, a machine configured to carry an ELINT fit that had been provided by the CIA in order to meet an Air Force requirement to determine the characteristics of the beacon transponder and the proximity fuse of the latest marks of the Soviet SA-2 Guideline surface-to-air missile deployed in Cuba. The concept for the 147D drone was that it would carry what is known as a travelling wave tube, a device that gave the 15 foot wingspan drone the radar reflective characteristics of a much larger aircraft and which, by thus acting as a decoy, would stimulate the Soviet-built radars in Cuba as it approached them. The radar and the SA-2 transmissions would then be picked up by a receiver in the 147D and transmitted down to a United States Navy ship suitably positioned outside Cuban waters. The D model was ready for operations in December 1962 but, at that point, the political and military situation in the Caribbean changed, and it was no longer possible to contemplate 'drawing up' an SA-2 for electronic inspection as had been intended. Nevertheless, the potential utility of unmanned aircraft had been advanced another step.

In the meantime, development work had continued on other models of the Ryan drone, notably the big-wing version 147B mentioned earlier, but with a new code-name, Lightning Bug, the old code-name Fire Fly having been abandoned when it was compromised. A model C was also used at this stage to develop and test the use of the Ryan Model 523 Doppler navigator, a system that provided cross-track error corrections to the autopilot of the aircraft.

By mid-1963, the general performance of the Ryan drones including the very important factor of their stability as camera platforms, led to the reconnaissance capability being declared operational with the 4028th Strategic Reconnaissance Squadron (Weather) of the 4080th Strategic Reconnaissance Wing at Davis-Montham Air Base Tucson, Arizona. Four Lightning Bug machines were assigned, two of the Model Cs and two Models D, as a temporary measure while the unit awaited the delivery of the new production Model B versions.

Within four days of the Gulf of Tonkin incident of 4 August 1964, which led to the American involvement in Vietnam, the unit from Davis-Montham was alerted and dispatched to Kadena Air Force Base on Okinawa, from whence it was planned that the Ryan drones would fly surveillance and reconnaissance missions over China and Vietnam. During September, several missions were attempted, with 147B drones being launched close to the coast of China and North Vietnam from C-130 aircraft (Figures 7.3 and 7.4) based at Kadena Air Force Base. The plan was that these drones

FIG. 7.3. Versions of Teledyne Ryan 147 RPVs uploaded for air launch operations. (*Photo: Teledyne Ryan Aeronautical*)

Fig. 7.4. DC-130A air-launch vehicle with Model 154 RPVs at wing stations before launch.
(*Photo: Teledyne Ryan Aeronautical*)

would carry out surveillance along the coast and over the interior of south-east China. To avoid restricted airspace in the area of Hong Kong, the drones were normally released South of the Colony to fly north-west to the Chinese mainland and then back to Taiwan. Recovery was made by parachute on the Island of Taiwan, only one-and-a-half hours flying time from Okinawa. The reconnaissance 'take' would then be flown back to Okinawa by T-39 aircraft, while the drones themselves were recovered to Kadena by C-130 aircraft. As an alternative forward base for recovery, Da Nang in Vietnam was designated, though it seems never to have been actually used for any of the missions out of Kadena.

These early operational missions by the 147 aircraft were all pre-programmed; there was no airborne remote control operator aboard the parent C-130 aircraft, nor any ground control apart from that used to direct the returning drone into its half-mile by two mile recovery area on Taiwan. The programming itself was achieved by using a pulse-Doppler system using a Doppler-signal update every seven miles against which the necessary flight events such as photographic 'takes', course changes and so on were pre-set before take-off. There was also a back-up system based purely on elapsed time, which meant, among other things, that accurate forecast winds had to be built into the flight programme before launch.

Many teething troubles were encountered during these operational missions. On the very first flight, one of the two drones mounted under the mainplane of the parent C-130 aircraft failed to unshackle for the launch, but then later in the flight unexpectedly fell off and, unpowered, glided down into the sea off Taiwan. Other drones were lost when they failed to respond to their command signals during the recovery sequence, or they simply crashed shortly after launch. Only two of the first seven missions were successful.

In an attempt to give the missions a 'cover', Nationalist Chinese insignia was painted on the drones before they left Kadena, but concealed by a patch that was removed immediately before take-off. Since several drones were lost over China, however, the origin of the aircraft would have been very clear to the Chinese from all the components that were obviously of American commercial origin.

After less than one month's operations out of Kadena, the group of United States Air Force and contractor personnel responsible for the flights were moved to Bien Hoa Air Base, 20 miles north of Saigon. It was, however, a short-lived attempt to move the unit to Vietnam. After eight days, the difficulties that were met at the ill-prepared base caused the unit to return to Kadena. It would be early October before a more permanent redeployment to Bien Hoa could be made. Although unserviceabilities and failures were still frequent, by 7 November seven successful reconnaissance flights had been flown by these unmanned aircraft.

The general pattern of operations in Vietnam was to proceed north-east out of Bien Hoa and over-fly Da Nang in order that the ground controller at that base could check that he had a good contact with the drone. Release was then usually effected well north of Da Nang, and the progress of the drone monitored by an Airborne Remote Control Officer in the parent C-130 aircraft, who would eventually acquire control of the aircraft during its return flight and hand it over to a Ground Remote Control Officer at Da Nang for final recovery.

By this time, the intrusions over China were provoking an appropriate reaction by the air defences of that country, and Peking reported accurately the first combat loss of a drone on 15 November 1964. By April 1965, five unmanned aircraft had been lost to the Chinese air defences and, in several cases, the wreckage was put on public display in Peking. The origin of the machines was obvious, but the United States authorities made no comment. These incidents demonstrated the clear vulnerability of drones with their steady flight paths and their inability to detect threats, much less to respond to them; but the most significant feature of the American losses was that clearly identifiable United States manufactured aircraft did not receive the same public attention as would have been the case with captured American crew members from, say, U-2 reconnaissance aircraft. Thus one of the principal advantages of the use of unmanned aircraft in hostile surveillance short of war was emphasised. Meanwhile, the Americans had not altogether abandoned manned reconnaissance. Indeed, U-2s were still being employed over North Vietnam, an area in which, at this stage of the war, the Communists had no SAMs with the capability to engage them. This benign picture was to change at the end of 1965 once Soviet-supplied SAMs arrived in North Vietnam and began to engage and bring down United States aircraft of all types, manned and unmanned.

As the Vietnam war developed, the number of unmanned aircraft employed by the Americans continued to grow. In October 1965, the first of fifty-six G-model versions of the 147 drone were delivered to the Air Force, gradually replacing the B models which had by now flown 70 combat missions. The average mission rate had been 2.6 per vehicle before the aircraft was lost either accidently or through enemy action, an encouraging start for an entirely new machine and a figure that would soon be bettered as the concept matured.

At this same time, two more Ryan models were placed under contract as the 147 programme expanded to include several refined marks (Figure 7.5). One was the H version, which retained the 1,920lb thrust T-41 engine. In order to give it still greater altitude capability, however, the mainplanes were extended from 27 to 32 feet and the wing area increased from 84 to 114 square feet. With additional fuel carried for

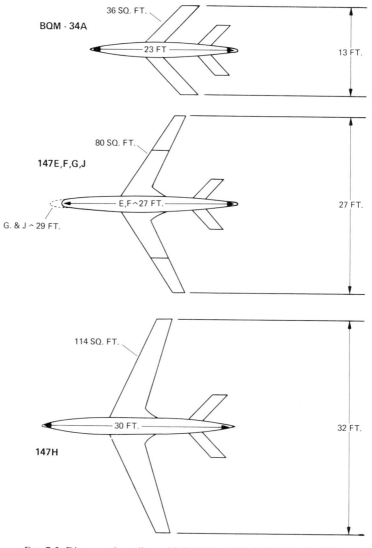

FIG. 7.5. Diagramatic outlines of BQM-34A, 147E, F, G & J and 147H

the first time in the wings, the H version also offered an extended range of 2,415 nautical miles, 960 nautical miles more than the G model. It was also the H version of the 147 that carried a newly-developed Microwave Command Guidance System (MCGS), to replace the original beacon/radio command system. It had been found that some of the South Vietnamese ground force communications systems had been interfering with the beacon/radio system, to the extent that three drones had gone out of control and been lost; the MCGS resolved this confliction. Finally, the operational equipment carried by the 147H included a new Hycon camera which was able to scan the very considerable area of 780 miles by 22 miles during a single mission.

A further version of the Ryan drone now placed under contract was the 147J. This was introduced as a low-altitude photographic version of the H, using the same 1,920lb thrust power plant. This machine was operational in March 1966, and it was a particularly noteworthy development because it employed, for the first time, a mid-air retrieval system (MARS) (Figure 7.6). It had been found that many

FIG. 7.6. MARS mid-air retrieval system. (*Photo: Teledyne Ryan Aeronautical*)

returning drones were being damaged as they landed by parachute into the Vietnamese countryside or even into the sea off Da Nang. Mid-air retrieval was not new, indeed it had been used on C119s and C-130 aircraft six years earlier to recover the payload of SAMOS and other reconnaissance satellites as they parachuted into the Pacific, but it was now to form a regular part of drone operations. The MARS system went into service with the drones in the Far East in April 1966. All told, 2,655 catches were made out of 2,745 attempts over the next few years, a remarkably high success rate of 96.7 per cent.

Two problems were now being encountered in the missions over North Vietnam. The first was the monsoon weather, whose overcast greatly inhibited photography; and the second was the twin hazard of SA-2 missiles, by then being installed more widely by the Communists, and the appearance in the war zone of Soviet-built MiG interceptor aircraft. One answer was to employ the earlier 147C drones fitted with a Barometric Low Altitude Control System (BLACS) to operate down to 150 feet, where they would not only evade North Vietnamese radar cover, but they would also be less affected by cloud, smoke and haze.

Thus, as early as October 1965, drones were operating in the high level and in the low level photographic reconnaissance roles; but by this time the increasing sophistication of the North Vietnamese air defences led to the requirement for an ELINT drone as well. This need was met at first by the 147 E, a development of the D model. In the 147E, all electronic transmissions picked up by the drone were converted to video or to Carrier-Wave (CW) level signals and then transmitted either to stand-off RB-47 aircraft or to monitoring stations on the ground.

The first operational launches of the 147E were made in the late autumn of 1965, but technical problems meant that the first successful flight against North Vietnamese defences did not take place until February 1966 when, although the first of the modified 147Es was shot down by an SA-2, it was able to transmit details of the missile guidance radar, the proximity fusing arrangements and of the barometric over-pressure that finally destroyed it. This Intelligence information proved to be invaluable, and it was held not only to have paid for the whole drone programme thus far, but also to have saved scores of American aircraft and crews in the years that followed.

In a further development of the Ryan family of drones, a single 147F version was produced by modifying one of the earlier B versions to carry an ALQ-51 ECM defensive package as well as a photo-reconnaissance fit. The drone flew two sorties, and on 22 July 1966 during its second mission the 147F was reported to have drawn ten or eleven SAMs before it succumbed to one of them. This was, of course, a very favourable ratio indeed of lost United States drones to expended North Vietnamese missiles, and demonstrated yet another valuable function for unmanned aircraft.

On 24 December 1965, the United States Government declared a pause in the continuing air attacks against North Vietnam, but continued the drone reconnaissance missions. This had the unwelcome result of allowing the Communist air defences to concentrate all their efforts on the unmanned aircraft, and the loss rate rose sharply. As a counter-measure, ten BQM-34A target drones were therefore hastily modified as the 147N model to act as decoys, which flew below the high altitude photographic drones, drawing the enemy fire. Eight missions were flown during March and April 1966, using this version of the Ryan family. All these expendable drones were eventually lost. The decoys had, however, proved their worth. Even though the North Vietnamese eventually became adept at distinguishing decoys from fully equipped drones, another ten of these unmanned machines, the further developed 147 NX version, were ordered for use in support of future B-52 raids against North Vietnam.

During these first two years of drone operations in South-East Asia, more than 160 missions had been flown, mainly by the 147G model. About one mission in six ended in the loss of the drone. By the Spring of 1966, the North Vietnamese claimed to have shot down 14, while Peking laid claim to another seven. In 1967, the drone programme was accelerated with 153 launches made, more sorties than in the whole of the previous two and a half years. These flights included not only missions by 147G, J and H and NX models but also by the later developments NP (low altitude day photo) and NRE (night reconnaissance electronic). In a further development, a fleet of BQMs was modified to the 147NA configuration (Figure 7.7), a version that dispensed chaff at medium altitudes from two external pods; and the 147NC model which was very similar except that it was provided with a different ECM fit. The urgency behind the deployment of these drones temporarily evaporated with the halt to all bombing north of the DMZ in November 1968. Although many successful exercises were flown in the United States, the NA/NC variant seems not to have flown on operations.

The year 1967 also saw the introduction of another significant version of these drones, the 147T, (also widely known as the AQM-34P), designed as the successor to the 147H. This model carried the same Hycon 338A camera as the H version, but it was fitted with a Continental J100-CA-100 engine giving it an increase in thrust of 45 per cent. It also had a greatly increased wingspan, which together made it possible for the aircraft to climb to 66,300 feet at 220 nautical miles from launch and to no less than 75,000 feet before the fuel supply ran out. The drone had an endurance of over four hours and it could photograph a 22-mile wide strip along 800 miles of track. Further refinements in the 147T included measures to reduce radar cross-section, and an ECM system designed to jam the guidance systems of North Vietnamese SA-2 missiles.

Up until 1969 no version of the 147 drone had been launched other than in the air; but in July of that year experiments began with the 147SK model, a ship-borne low-altitude day photographic reconnaissance drone which used Jet Assisted Take-off (JATO) bottles for its launch. Operational missions to evaluate the system were flown, with limited success, in the Gulf of Tonkin from the carrier USS *Ranger* in November and December 1969, with the drones under the airborne control of E2A aircraft. Further missions were flown in this way in the Spring of 1970. When the drones could be recovered the results turned out to be good. However, problems were encountered because of the difficulties of integrating the surface launch and parachute recovery of drones. Despite efforts to match the systems, the communications and the electronics of the drones were never fully compatible with those of the parent ship and no further sea-borne experiments seem to have been attempted.

On 18 April 1969, there was a further significant event in the Far East, when a Super-Constellation EC-121 Electronic Countermeasures aircraft was lost over the sea East of Korea. The aircraft had been operating out of Atsugi Naval Air Station near Tokyo on Electronic Warfare missions. These flights involved the deliberate stimulation of North Korean radar emissions so as to collect the transmissions for analysis. On that day, however, the presence of the Super-Constellation led not only to the activation of North Korean radars, but also to the launching of two MiG interceptors, which shot down the American aircraft with the loss of 31 crew members. President Nixon later admitted that 190 such flights had taken place in that area during the previous three and a half months, but this event brought the whole programme to an abrupt end.

However, this incident led directly to a proposal that the recently developed 147T should be used to carry a relay system by which electronic emissions could be collected and re-transmitted over an FM radio link to a ground station, thus obviating the risk of further losses to conventional aircraft and their operators. Four models of the resulting 147TE version were prepared for this mission, and the first operational flight was made in February 1970 from Osan in South Korea. Because of its high altitude performance, the 147TE was able to collect electronic intelligence from target facilities up to 600 miles from the ground control station. Twenty-two sorties were flown in the two months that this Operational Test and Evaluation programme was run, and then resumed in October 1970 with production models of the 147TE, by now known under the code-name Combat Dawn. Fitted with external fuel tanks, later models of the 147TE had a flight endurance of eight hours. With ten EW receivers on board, the machine could collect very large amounts of data. The aircraft was normally directed by ground control but it could also be controlled by an airborne DC-130 or it could be flown automatically to follow a pre-set programme.

The 147NQ version then followed early in 1968. This was a low-level development of the NX fitted with a high resolution camera. Instead of being controlled by a pre-set programme, it was directed by a controller in the parent C-130 launch aircraft, in other words, it was a true RPV, rather than a drone carrying an RPV over-ride facility. Sixty-six NQ missions were flown, mostly over Haiphong harbour and, in 57 cases, the RPV returned safely to base. The vulnerability of the drones against the constantly improving North Vietnamese air defences, particularly at low level, now led, however, to a new emphasis on survivability. The result was the quantity-produced S series of the 147. This version carried one camera instead of the

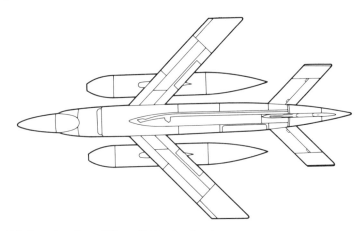

FIG. 7.7. Top plan view of TRA 147 NA showing the two external ALE-2 pods suspended beneath the drone's wings.

two fitted in earlier models, with the available film footage increased by 80 per cent and with the quality of the photography enhanced. Its survivability features included a Multiple-Altitude Control System (MACS) which offered three pre-selected flight altitudes between 1,000 and 20,000 feet that could be programmed into the drone at various stages in its mission. The SB variant also carried new rate-gyros in the yawing plane, giving more precise turns and a smaller turning radius.

It was the next version however, the 147SC (i.e. the AQM-34) that was to provide the largest production run of all the 147 series of drones and RPVs. Several hundred were built and, in all, they flew 1,651 operational missions. It had been expected that the SCs would average 2.5 missions each before before lost, but in fact they averaged 7.3 missions in operations in the Far East as a whole. This model of the 147 family was fitted with horizon-to-horizon cameras that took continuous photographic coverage along a low-level flight path of 155 miles and photographic resolution with the new system was reported to be as low as 1 foot. Accuracy on track was improved over earlier models by the use of cross-correlation Doppler radar. The mission was pre-planned through a digital on-board programmer which could, however, be over-ridden by a controller in the parent DC-130 aircraft. It was thus another hybrid RPV/Drone. At the end of its low-level mission, the SC was programmed to climb to altitude for the flight back to the recovery area, where the parachute recovery system would be operated and the drone collected in mid-air by a MARS helicopter.

The success of the 147s then led to the development of the night reconnaissance model, 147SRE, equipped with a Doppler navigation system and with an electronic flash system in the near infra-red spectrum, which made visual detection of the drone by hostile defences very difficult. Twenty of these machines were delivered.

The final months of the American involvement in Vietnam saw yet another role for the 147 family of drones, this time as leaflet carriers. The 147NA/NC (Figure 7.7) model was already equipped with external pods for carrying chaff, and it was a simple matter to substitute leaflets for the anti-radar metallic strips. Twenty-eight of these missions were flown between July and December 1972 as part of the Combat Angel ECM programme (Figure 7.8). At this latter date, however, a more active and a more crucial role became the focus of drone activity in efforts to gather EW material

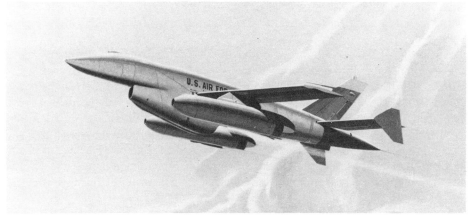

Fig. 7.8. Artist's impression of Teledyne Ryan AQM-34V 'Combat Angel' RPV (*Teledyne Ryan Aeronautical*)

preceding the attacks on Hanoi and Haiphong during the massive Linebacker II offensive by B-52 bombers. December 1972 became a period of considerable activity for drone operations, and in that month no fewer than 72 147SCs were launched, two thirds of them to survey the results of the concentrated air attacks against the North. By the time the subsequent cease-fire was signed on January 27th 1973, over 100 sorties had been flown in the previous 30 days. With the main and decisive air offensive now over, the United States announced that reconnaissance flights over North Vietnam would henceforth be limited to those at low level carried out by the model 147SC drone and to high altitude missions by SR-71 aircraft.

1972 had been the peak year for operations by the Ryan 147 family of drones. In the twelve month period, 466 missions were flown by 147SCs out of U-Tapao in Thailand, and many others were undertaken from other sites in the region as well as over the Sea of Japan. Virtually throughout the war in Vietnam from late 1964 until the ceasefire in 1973, the drones and RPVs of the United States Air Force had overflown China, North Vietnam and other areas of the Far East, making, according to some reports, a total of 3,435 sorties for a reported loss of only 4 per cent. It was a striking confirmation of the value of drones not only in generally hostile operational environments, but also on occasions against very determined enemy attempts to counter them during their deployment in the Far Eastern theatre.

OPERATIONS IN THE MIDDLE EAST

Meanwhile, events in the Middle East had led to considerable interest in other roles for drones. Since the Firebee had by now amassed such extensive operational experience, it was hardly surprising that this machine should form the basis of some further developments stimulated by events in the Arab-Israeli confrontation.

Interest in counters to the Soviet Styx anti-ship missile had been intensified by the loss of the Israeli destroyer *Eilat* to one of these weapons on 21 October 1967 (see page 55). 'Harpoon', a missile with a range almost three times that of the Styx, was still in gestation in America and would remain so for another five years. In the meantime, experiments were made with FLASH (Firebee Low Altitude Ship-to-Ship Homing Missile) in order to provide an interim capability of the kind offered by the Styx. This FLASH cruise missile was designed to fly at 300 feet, descending to 25 feet with a speed of 400 knots to deliver a warhead consisting of two 500lb bombs (Figure 7.9).

The original version was to be radar monitored and radio controlled to give corrections to the automatic programme, but later models were fitted with a TV camera. By the Spring of 1971, the system was developed and ready for test, using the Ryan BQM-34A as the vehicle. In April of that year, two of the drones were deployed aboard the destroyer USS *Anderson* for sea-worthiness trials. Live firings then took place in September 1971 using a DC-130 for airborne launch and the decommissioned USS *Butler* as a target. Very good results were achieved in the resulting demonstrations, but under pressure on procurement funds the United States Navy eventually abandoned this attack weapon in favour of the more effective Harpoon missile.

In another initiative to produce an attack system from the Firebee family, this time stimulated partly by the deployment of Soviet-built SAM and AA assets along the

Fig. 7.9. Teledyne Ryan Firebee releasing two 500lb bombs. (*Photos: Teledyne Ryan Aeronautical*)

Suez Canal in August 1970, a new model of the basic 147 was constructed using parts from a variety of existing versions. This became known by the Company designator, model 234 (Figure 7.10), and in December 1971 the first trial of the new drone was held.

The 234 was launched at 9,000 feet from a DC-130 and descended as programmed to less than 1,000 feet over the Nevada desert where it flew at 360 knots towards a simulated SAM site. The drone carried a TV camera in the nose, by means of which

FIG. 7.10. Teledyne Ryan Aeronautical Model 234 RPV uploaded with Maverick ASM is air-launched from DC-130. (*Photo: Teledyne Ryan Aeronautical*)

FIG. 7.11. Missile launched from a Teledyne Ryan Model 234 RPV hits its mark—a surveyed radar van. (*Photo: Teledyne Ryan Aeronautical*)

it was guided towards the target area. At about five miles range, the target—a radar van—was identified and the controller then switched to the optical seeker of a Maverick missile carried below the wing of the drone itself (Figure 7.11). At a range of two miles, the Maverick was fired and scored a direct hit on the van, the drone meanwhile being recovered for re-use. This was the first missile launch from a drone to score a direct hit.

FINAL DEVELOPMENTS IN THE FAR EAST

This success had coincided with renewed American air activity over North Vietnam at the end of 1971 and the loss of a significant number of United States aircraft heightened interest in the use of drones to suppress the Communist air defences. It was clear that drones could not carry out the complex missions of manned aircraft during the United States air offensive, but it was also clear that drones had a considerable potential to act as a first wave ahead of the attack aircraft. One difficulty, however, was that the North Vietnamese SAM sites were by now very skilfully camouflaged, even against surveillance by the human eye, and it was becoming virtually impossible to detect them by means of any electro-optical system such as TV. The result was a programme code-named 'Have Onyx' aimed at developing an infra-red detection system that could lock-on to the IR emissions of a SAM site, but once again the urgency of the requirement fell away as the United States involvement in Vietnam ended and this element of the 234 programme was not completed.

One of the most advanced models of the original Firebee series of RPVs at this time was the Model 255 (i.e. AQM-34V) which was, however, produced in 1976, too late for the war in Vietnam. This was a decoy machine designed to fly ahead of conventional attack aircraft, dispersing chaff and employing ECM to confuse hostile defences. It was controlled by DC-130H aircraft, each of which could 'parent' up to eight RPVs at a time.

Thus by the mid-1970s, unmanned aircraft had become an accepted and valuable contributor to warlike operations in the air. In the Far East in particular there was a pressing need for photographic and electronic intelligence on countries such as China which, while not at war with the United States, served as sanctuaries and as logistic bases for operations against the forces of the United States and its allies. Dispatching, and occasionally losing, unmanned aircraft on these missions led to little more than routine diplomatic protests from the target countries, in circumstances when the use of manned aircraft could easily have led to serious political embarrassment.

During operations in the combat zone of Vietnam itself, drones proved to be equally valuable in their reconnaissance role. Their activities not only produced high quality intelligence data, but also succeeded in drawing considerable fire from the Vietnamese defences that might otherwise have been directed at United States manned aircraft. The resulting losses to the drones were acceptable and of little consequence.

Most of the developments in drone technology during the period of the war in Vietnam were concerned either with improving the survivability of the machines, or with enhancing their intelligence collecting capabilities. But towards the end of the period, other operational possibilities were emerging, particularly including the use of drones in an attack role as launching platforms for air-to-ground missiles. Under the stimulus of crisis and war, the development of unmanned aircraft for use in combat had thus moved forward in several significant fields of utility.

ISRAELI EXPERIENCE

One other nation, Israel, has actively employed unmanned aircraft in war since 1973 at least. Israeli efforts centre on three machines; the Tadiran Mastiff, (Figure 7.12), the Israel Aircraft Industries Scout (Figure 7.13), and the later aircraft, the Mazlat Pioneer (Figure 7.14). Each of these is a miniature RPV and all of them are somewhat similar in operational concept. Pioneer and Mastiff can carry suites of equipment for electronic warfare, such as those for Counter Measures (ECM) and Electronic Support Measures (ESM), a laser designator or TV camera payloads, while the Scout is purely a surveillance platform equipped with a panoramic camera and a gyro-stabilised zoom TV camera, whose 'takes' can be relayed to a ground station.

In the field (Figure 7.15), a Scout operating unit is manned by a ground-crew of 12 and is equipped with up to eight of the RPVs together with a Ground Control Station (GCS), a launcher and a retrieving net into which the Scout is flown at the end of its mission. The power unit of the Scout is a 22hp two-stroke engine, the all up weight is 139 kilogrammes at take-off and the machine can carry a payload of up to 30 kilogrammes. The aircraft is guided in flight either by a pre-set programme linked to an autopilot, or by a controller in a GCS-2000 ground station vehicle operating a two-way data link. With a wingspan of only 4.96 metres and a construction that relies to a great degree on composite materials as well as on aluminium, the Scout

FIG. 7.12. Mastiff Mark III. (*Photo: Mazlat Ltd, Israel*)

Fig. 7.13. Scout Mini RPV. (*Photo: Mazlat Ltd, Israel*)

Fig. 7.14. Mazlat Pioneer. (*Photo: Mazlat Ltd, Israel*)

Fig. 7.15. A Scout MRPV about to be catapulted into the air from a pneumatically operated launcher. A tricycle version can take-off or land on any airstrip. (*Photo: Israeli Aircraft Industries Ltd*)

mini-RPV is not a prominent radar reflector, and this fact provides a very reasonable degree of invulnerability at the modest heights, up to 15,000 feet, at which the Scout operates. The top speed of the machine is 95 knots, the endurance seven hours and the maximum ground control range is 54 miles, in other words the Scout is a battlefield or tactical asset rather than a vehicle for strategic reconnaissance.

Mastiff is a twin-boom tactical RPV and it, too, is driven by a 22hp two-stroke engine. Like the Scout it makes a conventional take-off and is recovered into a net. It is controlled by VHF by the two-man crew in the GCS, where real-time data being collected by the aircraft is being continuously received and processed for display. Its payload can include a gyro-stabilised TV camera, a panoramic film camera, various EW and ECM packages, a laser designator, Forward-Looking Infra-Red (FLIR), and explosives. It can also be fitted with a radar lens so as to act as a decoy by simulating a larger conventional aircraft. The aircraft has a length of 3.3 metres, a span of 4.25 metres and a maximum payload of 30 kilogrammes.

The Mastiff and the Scout programmes were combined in 1984 to produce the Pioneer mini-RPV, and future production was undertaken by Mazlat Ltd. This aircraft is designed to carry a gyro-stabilised TV camera, but other payload packages including EW, ECM, decoy, range-finder designation and communications relay up to a maximum payload weight of 45 kilogrammes can be fitted. Pioneer is slightly larger than the Scout, but very similar in general appearance, and it uses the same composite materials and aluminium alloys to reduce the radar signature, but it is also designed to fly higher and to stay airborne longer than its predecessors.

In flight, the Pioneer is controlled by an autopilot and it is programmed to fly emergency evasive manoeuvres on command from its associated GCS. Throughout its mission the autopilot can be over-ridden by the crew in the GCS, where real-time data being collected by the aircraft is continuously received and processed for display. It is interesting to note that in another development, the Ground Control System has been split into separate Control and Communication functions, so as to reduce the vulnerability of ground personnel and their equipment to attack by Anti-Radar Missile (ARM) weapons.

But that takes the discussion beyond the actual operational use of unmanned aircraft by the Israelis, a feature of the Middle East conflicts that first emerged in the Six-Day War of October 1973. Because of Israeli insistence on secrecy, and because of the confused accounts that appear as the natural and intended result of disinformation generated by the Israelis, firm details are not available. But it does seem certain that in October 1973 Teledyne Ryan 124R drones were employed by the Israelis both on the Syrian front, and on the Egyptian front. Some were engaged as reconnaissance and surveillance platforms, and others as decoys. In both roles these machines seem to have been very successful, the reconnaissance sorties bringing back valuable raw intelligence, and the drones drawing the fire of Arab SAMs, thus causing the nugatory expenditure of valuable missiles and the weakening of Arab defences. In the case of one drone, it was reported that no fewer than thirty-two missiles were directed at it, and the drone was recovered undamaged; but this cannot be confirmed.

Rather more information, though still limited, is available on the Israeli use of unmanned aircraft during the air operations over the Bekaa Valley in 1982. Drones or RPVs, probably Northrop Chukar target drones, had carried out flights over the Bekaa as early as May in the previous year, not only in order to collect general intelligence, but also with the task of monitoring the reactions of the Syrian air defences to these and to other intrusions. The Syrians claimed to have shot down eight unmanned aircraft; the Israelis admit to the loss of five. According to some reports, more than seventy sorties a day were then flown by the Mastiff and Scout mini-RPVs on surveillance missions during the Bekaa operation itself. These flights included not only sorties over the Bekaa valley, but over Syrian air defence airfields. One report claims that the mini-RPVs were put on station over at least three airfields, using TV cameras to monitor runway activity and transmitting real-time information to the four Israeli E2C command aircraft employed, which in turn passed the Intelligence to the airborne Israeli combat aircraft so that they were able to make the successful interceptions that were such a striking feature of their victory over the Syrian ground and air assets.

It seems clear that other types of unmanned aircraft were also employed, notably Samsons and Delilahs. Samson was an air-launched unpowered glider designed to simulate the radar return of an F4 fighter. Because the Israeli attack on the Syrian SAM systems was launched at 1400 hours local time, the sun was behind the attackers, which meant that the Syrians were unable to acquire the incoming aircraft optically, and relied instead on their radars. The Samson drones stimulated the Syrian air defences, activating the fire-control radars and making them vulnerable to Israeli anti-radiation missiles, so that while the Syrians were launching their ready-use surface-to-air missiles at the decoys, the Israeli aircraft that were following them in were able to press home their attacks on the Syrian radars. The Samsons thus not only reduced the effectiveness of the Syrian anti-aircraft defences, but also made it far easier for the Israeli aircraft to neutralise those still posing a threat. Finally, it is also possible that the Israelis employed harassment drones to suppress radars such as the Gun Dish system of the Soviet ZSU-23-4 anti-aircraft gun, though again this cannot be confirmed.

What can be said, however, is that the Israeli success in this operation was complete. The Syrians lost virtually a complete air defence system in the Lebanon, including nineteen SAM batteries as well as 86 combat aircraft for the loss of only one Israeli machine. This overwhelming result can be attributed to several factors including careful Israeli planning and preparation, well practised combat skills, military equipment well matched to missions, a high degree of coordination and tactical adaptability. But an important part was also played by the imaginative use by the Israelis of unmanned aircraft, and while it is true that they did not—as some early reports suggested—explain the overwhelming Syrian defeat, they certainly prepared the ground for it and they made a substantial contribution during the combat itself. It may be, however, as in so many aspects of war, that in this very local engagement the pendulum of threat and response reached the extremes of its travel in the direction of the unmanned aircraft, and it is unlikely that we shall see this degree of surprise and its consequent success repeated in this way in any future conflict.

8
United States Cruise Missiles Revived

The revival in the early 1970s of American interest in cruise missiles had its origins in weighty politico-strategic factors. In November 1969, formal talks had begun between the United States and the Soviet Union on Strategic Arms Limitations, the SALT 1 talks. Agreement was reached by May 1972 on anti-ballistic missile systems and an interim agreement was also reached on strategic offensive weapons. The overall ceiling that was placed on nuclear weapons by this treaty meant that as the new American Poseidon-equipped submarines became operational, the older Polaris-armed boats would have to be withdrawn. But the treaty did not mention cruise missiles, and the Soviets were not prepared to negotiate about such systems since they had a monopoly in this class of weapons. There was thus a gap that the Americans might exploit.

The imperatives and the opportunities that then accelerated the emergence of this cruise missile for the United States Air Force can be traced to three factors. First, there was growing evidence in the late 1960s and the early 1970s of a constantly increasing efficiency in Soviet air defences. In particular, the Soviets had introduced a comprehensive variety of SAMs with overlapping areas of effectiveness that were likely to give entirely new levels of lethality in Soviet tactical, theatre and strategic ground-based air defences. This then led to serious concerns about the vulnerability of the American B1 bomber aircraft, particularly since there were doubts about the ECM fit that was intended to protect the aircraft in hostile airspace. One answer to this was again seen to be, as it had been in the case of the obsolete B-52, an air-launched missile that would be released outside the opposing terminal defences.

Second, and directly linked to the decision to develop cruise missiles, the cost of the new generation United States long-range bomber, the B-1, was itself under heavy criticism. At the start of the programme in 1970, the estimated cost of research, development and production for 240 B-1 aircraft was $9.9 billion. By 1977 the estimated cost had risen to $11 billion at 1970 prices, and it was expected to continue to increase. Eventually, in June of 1977, President Carter announced the decision to discontinue plans for production of the B-1, which he described as 'a very expensive weapons system conceived in the absence of the cruise missile factor'. Later he made clear 'the belief on my part that our defence capability using submarine-launched missiles and intercontinental ballistic missiles combined with the B-52 cruise missile combination is adequate'. The cancellation of the B-1 thus had the effect of accelerating the work that had already begun on ALCMs, and the United States administration made the decision to deploy about 3,000 of these weapons on the 151 B-52G bomber aircraft that were at that time in the inventory of the United States

Air Force. $3,000 million was therefore added to the Research and Development phase of ALCM development.

New Technologies

The third factor was that new technologies were making possible an entirely new concept of air-breathing missile that could be launched from well outside the worst of the enemy air defences to make their own way with great accuracy to distant targets. Above all in importance, new techniques in automatic navigation had been perfected which overcame one of the principal and most intransigent problems that had plagued all the cruise missiles developed hitherto, their lack of accuracy.

The new levels of accuracy that now became available were absolutely crucial to the success of the whole concept. The key lay in two associated techniques, Terrain Contour Matching (TERCOM) for strategic systems, and Digital Scene Matching Area Correlator (DSMAC) for tactical employment and for terminal guidance. The original TERCOM system had been patented in 1958 by the LTV-Electro Systems Company at a time when the radar map-matching techniques used in the Mace and Triton cruise missiles were being developed. TERCOM had been intended for use in the Chance-Vought SLAM cruise missiles, and attempts were also made to fit it into the Hounddog system. Both ventures failed, but TERCOM itself was to prove a very successful navigation system for cruise missiles.

Terrain comparison navigation techniques use a form of map in which variations in the height of the terrain to be traversed is converted into a digital presentation across a matrix of cells (Figure 8.1). For example, in the version produced by the E-Systems Company, there is a matrix of 64 cells, each of which covers an area of 400 feet square on the ground. Each square is allotted an average elevation which is then stored in

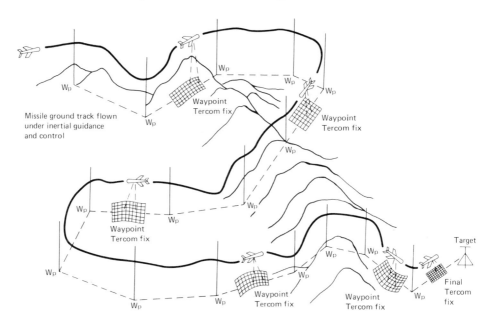

FIG. 8.1. Tercom Navigation.

the computer memory of the missile; relative elevations of as little as ten feet are reported to be employed by the system. The cruise missile carries a radar-altimeter which, by means of the computer, compares the reading it is taking from the terrain below with the digital map and determines what corrections are required—if any—to bring the two to match and thus to put the missile back on track.

It is not, however, necessary for the missile to make constant readings of this kind. The missile can depend on modern inertial platforms and their high quality gyroscopes to carry it with very good accuracy from one distinctive geographical feature to the next, features known as way-points, at which periodic up-dating is then carried out before the missile sets out on the next stretch of its path. These way-points can also be used to introduce changes in the heading of the missile so that it approaches its target in a series of zig-zags which are difficult for the defence to predict; or the missile can be routed so as to approach the target from an unexpected direction. Final updates close to the target itself can then be used to give good accuracy of impact, and certainly enough accuracy to satisfy the requirements for nuclear warheads. According to some reports, cruise missiles using the TERCOM system have been achieving an accuracy of between 100 and 600 feet. For conventional warheads, or in the case of nuclear warheads being directed against particularly hard targets such as ICBM silos or deep bunkers, some form of terminal guidance will be required, perhaps visual image matching or infra-red image matching.

Another important targeting technique is to supplement the input of TERCOM data with what is known as a Digital Scene Matching Area Correlator. Analogue and digital versions of DSMAC were trialled as long ago as 1979 in experiments comparing photographs taken in flight by the missile, with photographs of the target stored in an on-board computer. This system is claimed to be able to direct the missile to at least within tens of feet of its target, and perhaps even better.

Adding to the considerable attractions of these new techniques for navigation and guidance was the fact that by this same period, the early 1970s, the density of computers had been greatly increased by the use of solid-state and micro-circuit electronics and, in another crucial step forward, the size of inertial navigation systems had been drastically cut. At the end of the 1950s, such an inertial system could be expected to weigh perhaps 300lb. By 1970 the size, and the power needed for such a system, had fallen to such an extent that it could weigh as little as 29lb. The total cruise missile guidance package, consisting of inertial system, radar altimeter and computer, together weighed only 115lb and took up as little as $1\frac{1}{3}$ cubic feet of storage space. This development was little short of revolutionary.

A second invaluable technical contribution to the new possibilities in cruise missiles was made by improvements in propulsion technology. Developments that led to very small fuel-efficient jet engines had started in the United States in 1945, when the designers of the abortive United States Navy Gorgon projects had planned to use a jet engine with an outside diameter of only 9 inches. Work on the concept nevertheless continued after the cancellation of Gorgon, and by 1962 the Williams Research Company had produced the WR-2, an engine that delivered 70lb of thrust which was used to power small target drones such as the US MQM-74. By 1967, the WR-19 engine had demonstrated a thrust of 430lb for a weight of only 68lb and a fuel consumption of .7lb per hr per lb of thrust. This was a very good performance from an engine that was only one tenth the size of the next smallest available motor.

Even further improvements in propulsion were by now available through advanced fuels such as Shelldyne. Although much more expensive than conventional jet fuels, such as JP-4, fuels such as Shelldyne H have 33 per cent more energy per unit volume than JP-4 and they could give improvements in range for the cruise missile of about 10–20 per cent. Finally, and in addition to these striking improvements in navigation, guidance and propulsion for cruise missiles, nuclear warheads could also by now be miniaturised. The result was that, for the first time, very small, highly accurate, reliable and long range cruise missiles were at last a feasible option for the strike/attack mission.

NEW MISSILES

As early as mid-1972, the United States Navy had been examining a variety of proposals for a new cruise missile which included five different weapons and four launch options—some of them vertical and others firing from torpedo tubes and capsules. By the end of the year, the choice had narrowed to a Submarine Launched Cruise Missile (SLCM), eventually to be called the Tomahawk, designed to be discharged from standard torpedo tubes (Figure 8.2). This last specification was an important one because it restricted the weapon to a size of 21 inches diameter and 246 inches length, and it also put a ceiling of 4,200lb on its weight because that was the safe design strength of the torpedo handling equipment fitted in the submarines that

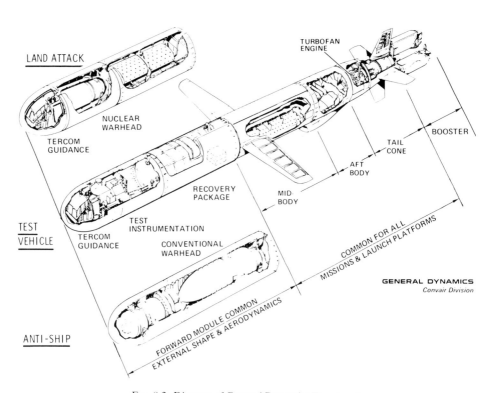

Fig. 8.2. Diagram of General Dynamics Tomahawk.

were to take the missile. The main role of the planned cruise missile was to be strategic, but there would also be a tactical option. Technologies developed for other systems were to be employed as far as possible and, for example, the engine from the SCAD programme and boosters from an anti-submarine weapon were adopted to the Tomahawk project continued into 1973.

In the United States Air Force, the SCAD programme had been cancelled on 13 July of that same year but the implications of the SALT discussions with the Soviets led Secretary of State Kissinger to stress the importance of the strategic cruise missile as a bargaining counter, and the Air Force programme, with Boeing as contractor, was revived under the nomenclature Air-Launched Cruise Missile (ALCM). There were thus two parallel programmes for cruise missiles. Under instructions from the Department of Defence, they were now brought closer together. In particular the Navy was to share the TERCOM navigation and guidance system with the Air Force, while the Air Force would reciprocate by sharing the technology of its SCAD turbo-fan engine and the advanced fuels that it used with the Navy. It was hoped that the resulting ALCM would enter operational service in late 1978, to be followed by SLCM in 1980.

For the Tomahawk SLCM programme, two contractors made bids, General Dynamics and Chance-Vought. General Dynamic's weapon was an 18 foot long missile with a wing-span of 8 feet 6 inches when the mainplanes were deployed from their scissor-style pre-launch storage position, in which one mainplane was mounted just above the other and sprung forward into the flight position immediately after launch. The missile weighed only about 1,000lb, was launched from a capsule and was powered in flight by a Williams F-107-WR-100 turbo-fan engine.

The Chance-Vought competitor was 20 feet 6 inches long including the booster rocket, and it carried an unusual one-piece 10 foot 6 inch-span wing, which was stowed along the axis of the missile before launch. After launch, the whole wing pivoted through 90 degrees about a central point into the athwartships position for flight. This weapon was powered by a Teledyne CAE 471-11 DX turbo-fan.

After a series of fly-offs, the Navy awarded the cruise missile contract to General Dynamics and the engine contract to Williams in March and May 1976. As the two cruise missile programmes progressed, there was continuing political pressure for further harmonisation between the system for the Navy and that for the Air Force, leading inevitably to renewed suggestions that one cruise missile should be made to meet both sets of operational requirements. The Air Force had maintained its reluctance to accept the Boeing ALCM as a weapons system in its own right, and until 1975 it continued to see the cruise missile as an adjunct to the B-52 bomber, with priority for its development well behind that accorded to the B-1 bomber and to the new United States Air Force Inter-Continental Ballistic Missile System, the MX.

But when it became clear in 1976 that Congress favoured the SLCM of the Navy, and that if there was to be any harmonisation of requirements, it seemed likely to mean standardising on the Navy missile, Air Force interest in the ALCM as a strategic system revived and work went ahead again in adapting the SCAD to produce it. This was not a particularly difficult transition since ALCM, like SCAD, basically had to fit the SRAM launcher of the B-52. SCAD and ALCM therefore looked much alike, with the same characteristic trapezoidal cross-section, and mainplanes that spread forward like a pair of switch-blades once the cruise missile

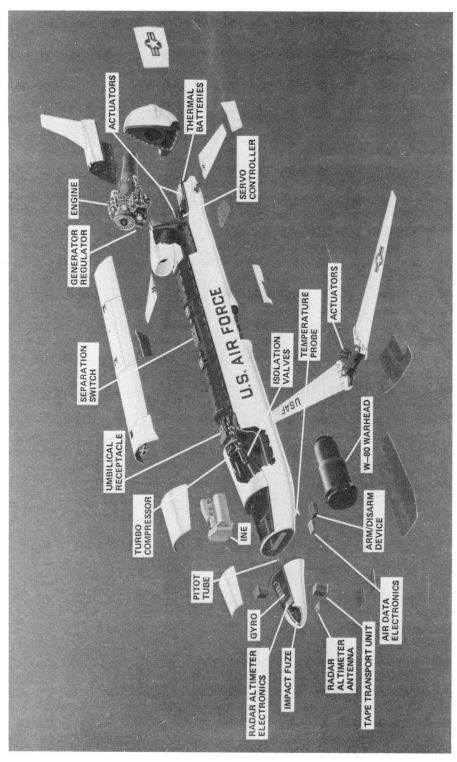

FIG. 8.3. AGM-86B ALCM exploded view. (*Boeing Aerospace Co.*)

was launched from the bomb-bay of the parent aircraft. The main differences between the two vehicles lay in the payload. Whereas SCAD had been designed to take an ECM package together with an array of 21 antennas, ALCM carried a miniaturised nuclear warhead (Figure 8.3).

Launching trials of the ALCM now went ahead in mid-1975. Flight tests began in March 1976 and on 9 September a Boeing AGM-86A air-launched cruise missile completed its first guided flight over a TERCOM range (Figure 8.4). Four map matrixes were navigated in a flight lasting 31 minutes, and carried out at heights varying between 180 and 30 feet above the ground; but owing to an error in fuel calculation the engine cut before the target was reached and the weapon crashed. Two further tests also then failed for different technical reasons. These set-backs and deficiences in the range capability of the AGM-86A now led Boeing to cancel the original version of the missile in 1977 and to substitute for it what was known as the Extended Range Vehicle (ERV) which eventually became the AGM-86B. It was a longer and a heavier weapon than the original ALCM, but more important, it would no longer fit the SCAD launcher.

Meanwhile, in September 1977, a competitive fly-off between the General Dynamics Tomahawk and the Boeing missile had been ordered by the Director of Defense Research and Development of the Department of Defense, to settle the question of whether the United States Air Force should be equipped with an airborne version of the SLCM or with the ALCM. The fly-off was scheduled to take place in May 1978, but was delayed for various reasons until July 1979. Between July 1979 and

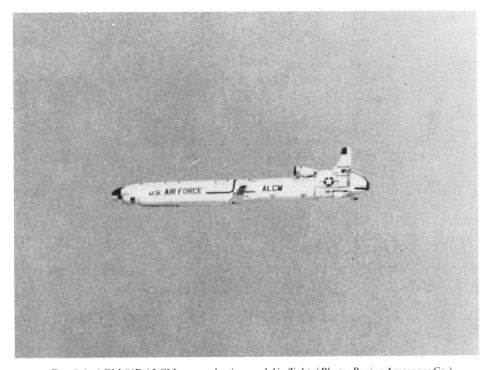

FIG. 8.4. AGM-86B ALCM pre-production model in flight. (*Photo: Boeing Aerospace Co.*)

February 1980 the Tomahawk SLCM then flew ten competitive sorties and suffered four crashes, while the Boeing ALCM made six successful flights out of ten attempts.

In terms of the fly-off, there was thus little to choose between the two systems, and since neither of them would now fit the SCAD racks of the B-52 aircraft this factor had also to be discounted. Eventually the Secretary of the Air Force chose ALCM over the SLCM for the United States Air Force and gave three reasons for his decision. First, the Boeing missile had demonstrated a better degree of TERCOM guidance. Second, the missile was likely to be cheaper and easier to maintain than Tomahawk. And third, the Boeing cruise missile had shown itself superior in its terrain-following capabilities. On 25 March 1980, therefore, he awarded a contract for 3,418 ALCMs to the Boeing Corporation.

More tests of the Boeing system now followed and they lasted until the mid-1980s. During that time various modifications were made to the ALCM, including cost-cutting changes in the materials used in its construction, and a cheaper but somewhat less efficient fuel than the expensive JP-9 used in the fly-off competition. Finally, in a significant departure from the original intention when ALCM was derived from SCAD, the extended missile was carried on external pylons instead of in the bomb-bay. Despite continuing reservations about the power-weight ratio of the cruise missile, which among other things meant a large turning radius in flight, the ALCM finally entered operational service with the 668th Bombardment Squadron of the 416th Bombardment Wing at Griffiss Air Force Base, New York in December 1982.

Meanwhile, the Navy pressed ahead with the Tomahawk SLCM. The first flight of the General Dynamics missile took place on 28 March 1976 and the first full flight test followed in June, three months ahead of the Air Force programme. In 1976 as a whole, Tomahawk flew sixteen test runs and, by now, the Navy missile had clearly overtaken the Air Force project.

Further development of the basic Tomahawk system for sea-launched roles now followed, leading to a family of three variants. The first is the anti-ship missile (TASM), which carries a 972lb blast and fragmentation warhead; the second is the conventionally armed land-attack version (TLAM/C) with either the same warhead as TASM or with sub-munitions; and the third is the nuclear-tipped land attack variant (TLAM-N) with a 200 KT yield. Each of the three variants has a different fuel-tank layout, guidance system and warhead; but because the engine and particularly the airframe with a length of 20 feet six inches and a diameter of 21 inches are common, all three versions can be discharged from the same launchers and in particular from the same standard submarine torpedo tube.

In its final version, Tomahawk is launched by means of a solid-fuelled rocket booster motor generating about 7,000lb of thrust. As speed increases from launch, the missile's wings deploy and a liquid fuel low-bypass turbo-fan engine, with a thrust of 600lb, takes over propulsion for the cruise element of the flight. The missile then flies en-route at about 470 knots maximum speed and at a minimum height of about 50 feet over the surface of the sea. TASM, the anti-ship variant, has a range of about 250 nautical miles and it is guided along its path by a Litton INS system. Terminal guidance is provided by a Harpoon missile seeker-head, modified to give a wider radar search pattern, an enhanced computer memory and a passive target identification capability. The missile can not only be tactically routed but can also be programmed to manoeuvre during the final phases of its flight so as to evade opposing anti-aircraft defences and to conceal the whereabouts of the launching platforms.

TLAM/C, the conventional land-attack model, and TLAM-N, the nuclear-tipped version, are reported to have a maximum range of 675 nautical miles and 1,350 nautical miles respectively. Each employs an inertial navigation system for the over-water phase of the flight only. As they coast-in over land, the TERCOM computerised terrain matching system is activated and calculates the necessary heading changes to be fed into the inertial navigation system. TERCOM checks are made periodically for the rest of the flight, the discrepancies theoretically reducing with each plot and terrain comparison until, in the case of the nuclear-armed version, the missile is brought to within a reported 100 feet of the target. In the case of the conventional version, the digital scene-matching correlator as employed in the Harpoon is used in the same way to match the target optically to the on-board memory characteristics, reportedly reducing the CEP to as little as three metres.

The account so far has dealt with four successful cruise missiles, the Boeing ALCM and the three variants of Tomahawk. There is also a fifth and important weapon that emerges from this somewhat complex background of operational, political, technical and budgetary factors, and that is the ground-launched cruise missile (GLCM). In fact, the missile employed for this role was another variant of the basic General Dynamics Tomahawk. The GLCM underwent development in the late 1970s and early 1980s, and in February 1981 the first successful platform launch was conducted. By June 1983, nine complete tests had been made with GLCMs, only one of which was a failure. These weapons are identical in all essentials to the Tomahawk, but they are deployed on 50 foot long transporter-erector-launcher (TEL) vehicles, cross-country prime movers weighing 78,000lb that are designed to carry four GLCMs each, mounted in capsules or containers and launched from the vehicle itself. The system is operated by the United States Air Force, who organise them into flights of four TELs and two launch centres, one a primary and the other a back-up control point. The TELs can be housed in, and the missiles fired from, hardened shelters on main bases, or the vehicles can be deployed and dispersed for survival in convoys consisting of 22 vehicles and 69 personnel.

There was one other operational off-shoot from these third generation United States cruise missiles, and that was the medium range air-to-surface missile (MRASM). Studies into such a weapon were initiated by the United States Air Force's Advanced Conventional Stand-Off Missile programme in 1975 and at about the same time by the Navy's Supersonic Tactical Cruise Missile project. A contract for the weapon was awarded to General Dynamics, this time without competition, specifying a terminal guidance system and a different payload of munitions from that carried by the much longer-range strategic cruise missiles. The result of the naval programme was another weapon very similar in appearance to the Tomahawk, though, in fact, the commonality of components amounted to only about 15 per cent. A payload of between 50 and 80 submunitions was carried with a total weight of up to 1,000lb, designed primarily for the mission of airfield runway neutralisation.

Several types of submunition were developed at the same time for this role. One version, the British JP-233, consisting of a mixture, first, of devices to penetrate the concrete of runways and then cause a 'heave' of the surface layers by a small underground explosion, and second, of anti-personnel devices to prevent runway repair. Another device was the Tactical Airfield Attack Munition (TAAM), which was a 13lb, two-charge munition that could be carried, sixty to eighty at once, by a cruise missile and scattered by individual parachutes over the target runway. A third project was the German STABO, which also employed a two-charge device, this time boosted by a downward firing rocket that drove an explosive-headed spike through the runway surface; and a fourth was the Boosted Kinetic Energy Penetrator (BKEP), which was very similar in principle. The Air Force eventually selected the BKEP for airfield attack, and other conventional warheads were produced for the anti-armour, anti-ship, anti-personnel, defence suppression, EW and reconnaissance roles. These munitions vary from the .42lb M-42, to the 990lb Bullpup fragmenting warhead and the 90lb BLU-73 fuel-air explosive device.

The equivalent missile for the United States Air Force, the AGM-109H (Figure 8.5) is yet another variant of the basic Tomahawk. It is 38 inches longer than that version and weighs another 700lb, including a payload of 1,200lb. Like the earlier versions of Tomahawk, it is guided by TERCOM and DSMAC. This missile, too, can carry a variety of warheads including the kinds of submunitions available to the MRASM version just described.

Other refinements for these advanced tactical cruise missiles are under way, many of them classified, but by 1987 it was known that they included an uprated engine both for SLCMs and for GLCMs that would produce an increase of 50 per cent in thrust yet give a reduction in specific fuel consumption. Incidentally, this availability of extra power might also be used to reduce engine observables, since most techniques with that purpose also have the effect of reducing available power from the engine. In a further improvement, the active radar ground-scanning TERCOM

FIG. 8.5. General Dynamics AGM 109 ALCM. (*Photo: General Dynamics*)

guidance system may be replaced by a passive system that would reduce or even eliminate the electronic emissions from the cruise missile.

DEPLOYING THE NEW CRUISE MISSILES

By 1979, NATO was considering a choice of four American theatre nuclear delivery systems for deployment into the European theatre, in addition to fixed-wing aircraft; these were ship, submarine, air and ground launched cruise missiles. The immediate stimulus for this development was that the Soviet Union had begun to deploy SS-20 missiles to replace their obsolescent SS-4s and SS-4bs, and NATO saw the need to redress the heightened imbalance of theatre systems with which the Alliance was now faced.

The older Soviet SS-4s and SS-5s were liquid-fuelled systems, which meant that they took some considerable time to prepare for launch, whereas the new solid-fuelled SS-20 could be held at immediate readiness. This also meant that during their lengthy process of preparation, the SS-4s and 5s were static and therefore vulnerable to pre-emptive strike or attack. The SS-20s were mobile and thus comparatively invulnerable. The SS-20 also had three other important advantages over the older systems: it was far more accurate, it was armed with multiple warheads, and the launchers (TELs—transporter-erector-launcher) could accept a reload. The SS-4 and 5 on the other hand were comparatively inaccurate, they had single warheads and they had only a single shot capability.

The important consequence of the Soviet SS-20 deployment was that the Soviets now had a highly effective first-strike theatre system with which Western Europe could be attacked from Soviet territory, whereas with the withdrawal of the United States Air Force F-111s and the Vulcan bombers of the Royal Air Force, there were no systems in Western Europe that could strike the Soviet Union. NATO thus faced the choice of relying only on its strategic nuclear systems, which would introduce an early and unwelcome escalation into the process of response, or of deploying advanced theatre nuclear systems of its own.

In looking at the options, NATO had to consider factors at two levels of discussion, the technical and the political. At the technical level, it was quickly appreciated that if the cruise missiles were carried in ships, then even heavily armoured surface ships would need to deploy so close to Soviet bases in order to fire their missiles that they would be vulnerable to Soviet offensive assets such as the Backfire aircraft. If the missiles were deployed on submarines, then in order to stay invulnerable to attack, they would need to launch their missiles from relatively deep water in the Western and Northern Atlantic, that is to say from positions at longer range from the Soviet Union than those from which, say, GLCMs could be operated. This meant a seriously reduced coverage of targets even in the western areas of the Soviet Union. Furthermore, although the dimensions of the SLCMs were explicitly such that they could be mounted in, and fired from, the conventional torpedo tubes of submarines, the limited number of submarines that could be made available for what was clearly a dedicated nuclear role, meant that the total nuclear throw-weight would be degraded, particularly when the vulnerability of cruise missiles in flight to defences such as Soviet look down-shoot down interceptor aircraft was taken into account. Finally, there was some unease about the blurring of distinctions between theatre and strategic systems that was implied in the use of submarines as cruise missile carriers.

As to ALCMs, although there were many attractions in air-launched systems, it was clear that if tactical aircraft such as Tornado were employed as carriers, then their commitment to the nuclear role could only be at the expense of their other and conventionally armed and more flexible roles. Put another way, if cruise missiles were deployed on to tactical aircraft, then those aircraft became as inflexible as the missiles themselves. Some flexibility in role was essential, and only these aircraft could provide it. This tended to outweigh the obvious advantages offered by these aircraft in their ability to penetrate at least some of the opposing defences before launching their ALCMs, and thus reducing the attrition levels likely to be suffered by the cruise missiles as they traversed hostile territory.

Another option was to employ longer-range aircraft such as the C130 Hercules transport. Large aircraft such as these would be too slow and too vulnerable to be able to penetrate or even to approach opposing defences, but their long range would enable them to operate from secure bases well to the rear and, perhaps more important, to select from a wide variety of launch points around the periphery of the Soviet land mass and thus exploit the weaker areas in the opposing defence systems.

These arguments seemed to point to a choice between GLCM and some kind of ALCM as the preferred option, and here a strong political aspect to the debate intervened. The European members of the Alliance saw the need for an effective United States theatre nuclear commitment that was physically deployed on European territory if any suggestion of decoupling Western defence from United States strategic nuclear assets was to be avoided. At the same time, the West German Government was anxious that the risk implicit in such a European basing should not be confined to that country but that other European states such as Holland, Belgium and Italy as well as the United Kingdom should accept whatever system was selected.

The pressures for a physical American nuclear presence in Europe clearly favoured the use either of Pershing ballistic missiles—which was another possibility—or of Ground Launched Cruise Missiles; but since even the extended range of the Pershing II was only about 600 miles, this meant that targets in the Western USSR could not be reached from launching sites in the United Kingdom. Only GLCMs with a range of about 1,700 miles would meet both the demands for an American presence and the policy of split-basing. It was therefore decided that GLCMs would be the system deployed, and that they would be based in the United Kingdom, the Federal Republic of Germany, Belgium, Holland and in Italy. But because it was also the case that the up-rated Pershing II would fit more easily into a basing and operating pattern that was already familiar and accepted by West European military and civil authorities, it was agreed that Pershing would also continue to be deployed in continental Western Europe.

So far as unmanned aircraft were concerned, the resulting arrival of GLCMs on bases in Western and Southern Europe was probably the first occasion since the V1 campaign of 1944 that cruise missiles of any form had been deployed in so comprehensive a fashion. The striking changes in technology that had taken place over the intervening four decades had meanwhile changed the threat potential involved from a crude, modestly powerful random weapon into one that combined extraordinarily high destructive capacity with remarkable accuracy of delivery.

9

Concepts of Manned and Unmanned Aircraft

As was pointed out at the start of this volume, unmanned aircraft form only one branch of the wide family of vehicles and missiles that makes use of the air environment in war. To assess the place of unmanned aircraft in operations we need to consider questions such as the relative cost and utility both of manned and of unmanned systems.

Manned aircraft are very expensive and their unit cost is still rising. Indeed, the rate of cost increase of all major items of combat equipment from one generation to the next is very striking. For example, the Type 22 Frigate of the Royal Navy costs three times as much in real terms as its predecessor, the Leander class. The MCV 80 Armoured Personnel Carrier is three-and-a-half times as costly as the vehicle it replaced in the British Army, the FV 432 series. The Seawolf missile fitted to ships of the Royal Navy costs over three times as much as the weapon it replaced, the Seacat. And even the L15 HE artillery shell of 1980 is twice as expensive as the 5.5″ HE round of 10 years before. The pattern of costs for aircraft is very much the same. In the case of United States aircraft for example, the P-51 of 1944 cost (all at 1985 prices) less than £300,000; the F-100 of 1954 cost just over $2 million; the F-4 Phantom in 1962 cost just over $6 million; while the F-15 of 1974 cost $25 million. The United Kingdom experience is not dissimilar. For example, the Harrier GR1 of 1970 cost four times as much as the Hunter F6 fighter of the 1950s, and the same trend is seen even in training aircraft; the Hawk, for example, costs one-and-a-half times as much as its predecessor, the Gnat.

The costs of weapons for air warfare, too, have greatly increased over the years. The standard 1,000lb bomb of the Second World War would, at current prices, cost about £2,000; but the present Maverick ground attack weapon costs £300,000 and the JP233 airfield attack weapons cost almost £500,000 each. Across defence equipment as a whole, the unit production cost historically rises at an average rate of just over 8 per cent per year over and above the annual inflation rate. If that Relative Price Effect, as it is known, is extrapolated it means that the real cost of a new aircraft in 25 years time will be more than six times the cost today.

Nor is it only the production cost of aircraft that is rising in this way. As a rough rule of thumb, the cost of in-service support for an aircraft is about twice the production cost, and the cost of that support is also increasing. Statistics from Tactical Air Command of the United States Air Force show that the cost of replenishment spare parts during the in-service life of an F4E aircraft is $3.5 million, and for an F-15A it is $10.7 million, while the depot maintenance costs for the same aircraft are $7.7 million and $5.8 million respectively. The total in-service operational and support costs for one aircraft, including all items such as fuel, pay for unit personnel, pay for indirect support personnel, support equipment and so on work out at $66.4 million and $64.2 million respectively for the two types.

Personnel costs are also high. Combat fighters in the United States Air Force inventory now need an average of 17 maintenance specialists for each machine, and a detachment of 24 F-15s for a 30 day period calls for 621 maintenance specialists in 22 different trades, together with 370 short tons of equipment. The aircrew are a particularly expensive item. In the case of the Royal Air Force, the cost of training a pilot for fast-jet aircraft such as the Harrier or the Tornado is almost £3 million at 1987 prices.

And finally, there is the cost of the training organisation itself. Historically, the proportion of training aircraft to combat aircraft in a modern air force has always been high. In the case of the Royal Air Force for example, in 1945 there were 8,745 aircraft in operational units, but another 15,857 in training units of one kind or another. From that peak of wartime activity, the huge training machine wound down to a more normal peacetime establishment so that by 1958, and after drastic cuts in the Royal Air Force in the previous years, the figures were 1,249 operational aircraft and 1,473 in training units. By 1969 the figures were 723 operational aircraft and 860 aircraft in training units with another 155 in communication and miscellaneous units. After more years of cuts in resources and further searches for economies, the figures for 1987 are 758 operational machines, 833 in training units (but including Operation Conversion Units which also have a war role), and 31 aircraft in communication units. The categories are complex and the figures are not directly comparable; but the trend is clear and the resources absorbed by training are obvious.

Because of the entirely different concepts involved in unmanned as compared to manned aircraft, no sensible balance of cost-effectiveness can be drawn. But it must be stressed that unmanned aircraft are certainly not cheap, and their cost is an important factor when their place in warfare are considered.

The American Aquila system, for example, was reported to be costing close to one million dollars per vehicle in 1986, while the whole programme of four batteries, with an inventory of 84 of these RPVs, was projected to cost between $2,000 million and $2,500 million. In the case of American Cruise Missiles, the marginal cost of 95 GLCMs (that is to say the cost of the additional buy, ignoring all the earlier expenditure on research, development, establishing the production line and so on) was quoted in 1986 at $100 million. Similarly the marginal cost of 249 Tomahawks was given as $670 million, or nearly $2.7 million each. To these costs for unmanned aircraft must be added the cost of their ground support equipment such as sensors, particularly for RPVs, which, according to some sources, can account for as much as 75 per cent of the whole system, including the personnel and all the expenditure on training.

In general, it can be said that if a particular unmanned aircraft is designed to be simple, limited in role and recoverable, as in the case of tactical reconnaissance vehicles like the Israeli Scout vehicle, then its cost effectiveness can scarcely be in doubt. But if the unmanned aircraft is more complex, larger and thus more vulnerable; if it requires skilled controllers and other expensive support; or if it is explicitly a one-way vehicle, such as a conventionally-armed cruise missile, then its cost-effectiveness compared with manned aircraft that can carry out repeated, varied and complex missions, is by no means easy to judge.

The balance will depend very much on the military importance attached to the mission, the availability of the various systems, and the effectiveness of the opposing defences, among many other considerations. In other words, the fact often stressed that an unmanned aircraft is undoubtedly less expensive than a manned machine, copy for copy or system for system, is only one element in a very complex picture. And it is a picture in which, as will be discussed, the basic mission requirements to be satisfied play a far more important part.

In yet another complicating factor in this whole question of cost and effectiveness, the trend that was discussed earlier towards higher prices of manned aircraft and the consequences of their apparently inexorable rise is now being mitigated in two significant ways. One is that the number of aircraft types in national air force inventories has been reduced. In the Royal Air Force, for example, the period 1950–60 saw no fewer than twenty new types of aircraft introduced to service. The next decade saw only five; 1970–80 brought four new types and the decade 1980–90 will see three. This trend has concentrated resources on to more economic production runs, a process helped to some extent by the longer runs implicit in international procurement such as that for the tri-national Tornado aircraft. But for that, the cost of front-line aircraft would have been even higher than they are.

The second amelioration is coming from an increased emphasis on Reliability, ease of Maintenance and ease of Testing, known as RMT, in efforts not only to cut the heavy cost of in-service support but also to increase the combat readiness of the available weapons systems. The difficulty with RMT initiatives is that the design, development and production needed to ensure those qualities all demand investment at the earliest stages of the procurement process in the expectation of support cost savings during the life-cycle of the weapons system. Yet the trade-off can never be quantified, and significant investment in RMT at a stage of procurement when many other and often conflicting demands are being made, calls for an act of faith that many operators are reluctant to make. Put more crudely, the cost of the required RMT investment is often translated into a larger initial procurement of systems and the consequent high cost of in-service support is left for later solution. The fact is, however, that pressures on resources seem certain to make RMT investment in complex air weapons systems increasingly attractive in the future.

Effectiveness

Those considerations tell us something about the abatement of rises in unit costs and in support, but the increased costs of modern systems are strikingly offset by another key factor, that of operational effectiveness. Some idea of the improvements that have been made in this field can be gained from a comparison of factors such as weapon loads, accuracy of delivery and sortie-rates.

As to weapon loads, a fighter bomber of the 1940s might carry two 100lb bombs, but by 1955 the Super-Sabre F-100C could carry 6,000lb of stores, and by 1974 the F4 Phantom was carrying eleven thousand pounds of bombs as well as gun-pods and rockets. Three years later the United States Air Force A10A Thunderbolt was in service with a maximum payload of 18,000lb of external stores, or over one-and-a-half times the maximum bomb load of a Lancaster aircraft of 1944, and over four times the bomb load of a B-17 bomber operating typically against Berlin in 1943.

Of even greater significance is the accuracy with which these higher payloads can be put on to their targets. Bombing inaccuracies were a notorious feature of the Second World War, and, for example, in 1941 a study by Bomber Command of the results of one hundred typical bombing raids showed that only one in three bombers claiming to have attacked targets in Germany was hitting within five miles of the aiming point, that is to say in an area of 75 square miles around the target. During that same war it required an average of something like 800 bombs, with all the repeated sorties that this implies, to destroy a single tank.

Over three decades were to pass before any decisive progress was made in eradicating this area of serious weakness in air power application. As late as 1972, for example, American aircraft had expended a very considerable weapon load in approximately 700 sorties against the Than Hoa bridge in North Vietnam using free-fall bombs, but without success. The bridge was eventually brought down by a single 3,000lb bomb put on to the target with laser-guidance. Many similar instances of extreme accuracy followed during the final stages of the war in Vietnam, and this new effectiveness of air power was clearly shown again in subsequent engagements in the Middle East. In particular, the Israeli Air Force demonstrated a notable level of accuracy both in its attack on the Iraqi nuclear plant at Tuwaitha near Baghdad in June 1981, and against PLO HQ in Tunis in October 1985. In the same general Middle Eastern theatre in April 1986 the United States Air Force carried out highly successful attacks on targets in Libya not only with similar very high precision, but from low-level and at night.

In many areas of warfare, single-shot kills by missiles are commonplace, and it is not going too far to say that if a target can be seen and acquired by a sophisticated guided missile, then it can be neutralised. The combination of close and virtually continuous target surveillance, usually by satellite reconnaissance, reliable target acquisition and above all weapons that can home on to targets or be directed on to them with extreme precision, has now given an operational effectiveness to relatively small numbers of aircraft that has transformed the airpower scene. This new operational leverage of air power has, against most targets, halted and then reversed the loss of impact that was being caused by diminishing numbers of combat aircraft.

One other important factor has also played a part in this process, and that is the development of new warheads for weapons. One of the most impressive developments in warheads over the last two decades has been the improvement in armour penetrability. The latest shaped-charge warheads for example can, in ideal conditions, penetrate a thickness of conventional armour up to nine times the diameter of the shaped charge itself. Another field in which important progress is being made is that of homing submunitions. Armoured vehicles such as tanks carry most of their armour where, up until recently, the anti-armour threat has shown that maximum protection is needed, that is to say at the sides of the tank, on the turret and particularly on the front or glacis plate of the hull. The result of this is that a tank such as the Soviet T-55 has, because of the slope of the glacis plate, a horizontal shot-line thickness of 200 millimetres. But because the tank designer must save weight wherever he can, and because the only threat to the top skins of tanks had up until recently been artillery fragments, a top armour thickness of only 20–40 millimetres is not uncommon. Homing sub-munitions are now being developed that can take advantage of this kind of weakness. Other warheads have been designed for specialist tasks such as penetrating concrete shelters, and a further particularly significant field is that of anti-airfield weapon such as the JP 233, which has been developed to break up the concrete operating surfaces of enemy airfields, and to sow anti-personnel sub-munitions so as to hinder repair work.

Thus, although manned aircraft are very expensive, those costs are increasingly being balanced by much higher cost-effectiveness derived both from more economical capital investment and from higher weapons system efficiency.

CONCEPTS OF AIR POWER

Mobility

The discussion of cost and effectiveness introduces the wider subject of air power concepts and the place of unmanned aircraft within those concepts. Basically, air power is about the high mobility and the operational reach of aircraft, qualities that can be exploited in a variety of ways; for example to concentrate for effect or to disperse for survival. And it is in these fields of military considerations that the advantages of manned and unmanned aircraft diverge, since unmanned aircraft cannot so easily transfer their effort between bases. They must be transported from one operating site to another, whereas a manned combat aircraft is itself the means of transport. And if they are to arrive with the urgency that contemporary operations demand, then transport aircraft will be needed to fly them on to relevant bases, or else they will require carrier aircraft from which they can be launched on their missions. In both cases, the apparent economies implied by the relative simplicity of the unmanned aircraft can be outweighed by the demands for airlift or airborne support.

Aircraft can also have a valuable part to play in crisis management. They can be deployed in ostentatious alert postures, for example on operational readiness platforms near the end of runways, both as a signal of intent and of readiness, thus giving politico-military warning to a potential opponent either by means of the satellite surveillance that he can be expected to maintain, or simply by giving international publicity to the fact.

Alert Postures

Manned and unmanned aircraft can both be used in this way to signal intention of warning, but the advantage of manned aircraft is that their deployment at alert status can, if necessary, be concealed among routine peacetime training missions. The deployment of, say, ground-launched cruise missiles during a crisis is unambiguous and perhaps provocative to an adversary, while being equally unambiguous and perhaps alarming to the domestic population.

Once manned aircraft are actually launched in a crisis or in an operational environment, there are still various options open to the command authority. The aircraft can be directed to proceed to its target, or it can be held in an airborne pattern so that it evades any pre-emptive strike on its base by, for instance, enemy missiles, yet it remains available to proceed to the target if and when ordered; or it can proceed towards the target and be given revised instructions in the light of late Intelligence while it is en-route. This option shortens the time taken to reach the target once final clearance is given and may offer some flexibility in crisis management, since it could enable the command authority to recall the aircraft from its mission if that course of action became either prudent or imperative, though it must be said that the time-frame implied, together with the likely effects of enemy electronic warfare capabilities, make this a less attractive advantage than it was once held to be. Thus the fact that an aircraft takes far longer to reach its target than does a ballistic missile, can in some circumstances actually be an advantage. Suitably designed RPVs can easily give the same advantages at less cost and no risk to crews; but in the case of a cruise missile, if it is not launched it may be destroyed by a pre-emptive attack; once launched, the missile is committed either to its target or, if it is so equipped, then to self-destruction in flight on command from the launching authority.

When air power is engaged between theatres of operations, rather than within a single theatre, mobility can be exploited in two ways. It can be projected from the home base into the airspace of a distant theatre, but making no use of ground facilities in the target theatre. Or conventional air power can be actually deployed into the theatre by transferring air assets, together with their support for local employment, an option that thus makes available in the new theatre all the qualities of air power. Because of the technical difficulties of maintaining control of unmanned vehicles over anything but modest ranges, particularly in a hostile environment, it is difficult to see how RPVs can have a useful role in inter-theatre operations unless again they are supported by airlift or air-launch; but drones, and in particular long-range cruise missiles clearly can have a very important part to play in stategic operations.

Historically, deployments of air power into theatres have been more common than projections of air power from a distant theatre. Although the logistic penalties of setting up in-theatre support facilities whether for manned or unmanned aircraft are likely to be considerable, and although the in-theatre bases and support facilities may be less secure because they are then within closer reach of the opponents, the advantages of rapid reaction, and in the case of manned aircraft sustained effort and of payload delivered, are usually overwhelming.

Flexibility of Role

Flexibility is a particularly important quality in air warfare, and one that has two separate aspects in military aircraft; role flexibility and combat flexibility. Role flexibility is concerned primarily with matching weapons to targets. Many modern combat aircraft are constructed so as to be able to carry a wide variety of weapons, which can range for example from guns, either integral to the airframe or mounted in pods attached to the aircraft, to nuclear devices, to simple gravity bombs, guided bombs, guided missiles for a variety of specialist roles and sub-munition dispensers, to less lethal but operationally vital stores such as reconnaissance cameras, ECM pods, chaff dispensers and IR flares. The same kind of flexibility can also be built to some extent into unmanned aircraft, so that drones and RPVs can carry weapons, ECM fits, chaffs and so on. The limitations on the variety of payload in unmanned machines, and on the size of that payload become less important if the high cost of manned aircraft can be balanced by making available much larger numbers and various models of much cheaper and perhaps less expendable unmanned craft.

Combat flexibility is essentially about the ability of an aircraft to deal with changing operational circumstances in the air; in other words it exploits the features of an aircraft once it is launched. Combat flexibility makes use of manoeuvrability, speed, passive protection devices, and active defences; but above all it relies upon the tactical skills of the crew and their ability to react to immediate circumstances, or their 'situational awareness' and their ability to fight their aircraft. It is in this area of combat flexibility that the operational characteristics of manned and unmanned aircraft perhaps most sharply differ, and these differences are discussed in some detail in the final Chapter, both in terms of pre-programmed unmanned aircraft, and in terms of remotely piloted air vehicles.

10

Present programmes

As the introduction to this volume in the Air Power series made clear, it is not intended to offer a catalogue of all the numerous unmanned aircraft projects that are in existence. There are specialist publications available to do that, but in any case it is an aspect of aeronautics in which many projects emerge only to disappear again in a short space of time. This chapter deals with some of what appear to be the main contenders for future operational roles. Above all, it draws out the significant directions in which progress in unmanned aircraft as a whole seems to be moving.

A survey of the non-Warsaw Pact unmanned aircraft by the American magazine Aviation Week and Space Technology in March 1987 listed no fewer than 58 drones and RPVs in development or in production in the United States alone. A closer examination of the vehicles concerned, however, suggests that there is only a limited interest in the operational potential of these machines. Of the 58 aircraft described, 36 were designed exclusively as targets; the Northrop Chukar (Figure 10.1) is a good example. Another thirteen vehicles had a surveillance, reconnaissance or target

Fig. 10.1. BQM-74C CHUKAR III Aerial Target. (*Photo: Northrop Corp.*)

acquisition function, two were described as having multi-roles which included EW, and four were designed for research for civilian use or for aircraft recognition training. Two models had harassment or decoy functions, and only one of the 58, the E-200 manufactured by the Melpar Division of E-Systems Inc, claims to have a strike or attack role. The same survey also covered non-United States programmes, and here 29 unmanned systems were listed; 18 were concerned with target drones or RPVs, and nine were reconnaissance or target acquisition systems. There were no attack or other combat vehicles listed.

It seems clear from samples such as this that the current interest in unmanned aircraft is overwhelmingly connected with their value as target drones of one kind or another, an interesting confirmation of one of their original roles during the earlier decades of this century. Next in importance is the mission of surveillance and reconnaissance, and this should not surprise us. The advantages of such systems are clear. First, a combination of lightweight engines, miniaturised electronic components, control systems and stabilising gyroscopes together with high quality optical and television equipment has made possible the construction of small signature surveillance aircraft at very modest cost. The Northrop BQM-74C is a good example of an advanced unmanned aircraft of this kind (Figure 10.2).

Fig. 10.2. BQM-74C/Recce. (*Photo: Northrop Corp.*)

Quite apart from these technical factors, it is also the case that the use of such machines in high-tension areas not actually at war, as for instance in the Middle East, has become little more objectionable than the regular overflight of surveillance satellites. If manned aircraft were to be employed for reconnaissance in those circumstances, then on the one hand there would be stronger international reaction, and on the other there would exist the very real possibility of political embarrassment caused by the loss or capture of the crew.

Where actual war fighting is concerned, unmanned reconnaissance aircraft have shown themselves capable of several of the functions hitherto carried out by conventional aircraft, yet the demands on resources in terms of manpower and equipment are less, and the loss of skilled crews is avoided. Far more important in an era when air power assets are less plentiful than they were, say, three decades ago, the use of unmanned reconnaissance machines releases conventional aircraft for other roles and thus acts as an important force-multiplier.

The detailed operational requirements in the West for the development and procurement of weapons systems, including combat aircraft, are often driven by concepts within NATO. In the case of unmanned aircraft, there is only pressure for a limited number of programmes that are presently funded or contemplated. However, three distinct roles have been identified within NATO for the future employment of RPVs. These are; first, medium range surveillance, reconnaissance and target acquisition; second, defence suppression, using the RPV either as an ECM platform or as a hard kill weapons carrier; and third, an anti-armour RPV for battlefield interdiction.

The last two functions are still in the concepts stage, though the Northrop Tacit Rainbow anti-radar drone, described later, is now showing promising progress. For the medium range surveillance mission, there are at least two current contenders, the GEC Phoenix and the Lockheed Aquila.

The primary task for the British Army's Phoenix system (Figure 10.3) is the

Fig. 10.3. GEC Reconnaissance Vehicle. (*Photo: GEC Avionics Ltd*)

detection, recognition, identification and location of targets for weapons such as the Multi-Launch Rocket System. Its secondary functions are those of locating targets beyond the Forward Edge of the Battle Area, and general surveillance. The aircraft is designed to penetrate up to a depth of 50 kilometres in hostile airspace and it will operate in all weather and in darkness. Possible payloads include decoy equipment, and ECM fit and a laser designator, as well as a thermal imaging sensor.

Aquila (Figure 10.4) first flew in 1975 as part of an RPV demonstrator programme, and some 23 were built up to 1978. Development was resumed in early 1986 when it was shown that despite earlier disappointments with the system, Aquila was able to satisfy the detailed criteria laid down by the United States Army for an unmanned reconnaissance and laser designating system that would be mobile and survivable on the modern battlefield.

The Aquila payload of less than 60lb includes a TV camera, a laser range finder/designator and automatic video tracking. Eventually it is intended that the vehicle will carry a forward-looking infra-red system developed by the Ford Aerospace Company. The aircraft is powered by a 26hp engine driving a 26 inch diameter propeller within an annular ring empennage. Aquila is launched by hydraulics from a truck-mounted ramp and it is controlled in flight by a digital autopilot and strapdown inertial attitude reference sensors. Navigation is effected by means of dead reckoning updated by jam-resistant transmissions from ground control. The pre-programmed flight of Aquila covers launch, en-route navigation, search orbit patterns and recovery, this latter carried out by means of a truck-mounted net. It seems clear that the Aquila has some potential for further development, though its future capability is inhibited by the line-of-sight limitation to its range. This, and the several other disadvantages that are present in the whole concept of unmanned aircraft are discussed later in order to illustrate some of the practical problems and difficulties that need to be dealt with if unmanned aircraft are to be operated in combat conditions.

FIG. 10.4. Lockheed AQUILA Reconnaissance Vehicle. (*Photo: Lockheed Corp.*)

Outside those projects designed to meet specific Alliance requirements, there are several other ventures that will serve to illustrate the present state of development in this branch of aeronautics.

One current programme by Teledyne Ryan is their quarter-scale Mil-24 Hind D Soviet helicopter powered by a 50-HP microlight engine, and originally intended purely as an inexpensive AA target. But interestingly enough this small aircraft is now also being studied as a prospective vehicle for tactical reconnaissance. The Teledyne Ryan Model 328 RPV by contrast was developed as a reconnaissance vehicle from the outset. This miniature and recoverable aircraft began tests in early 1985. It is only 10 feet 3 inches long with a wingspan of 11 feet 10 inches, and it has a cruising speed of 70 knots. Its endurance is about seven hours at typical operating heights of between 3,000 and 10,000 feet. The first versions of the Model 328 carry infra-red line scanning equipments, but surveillance by TV camera and the role of EW jamming are also being considered for the aircraft.

At the time of writing, 1988, Teledyne Ryan have also been working on a high-altitude long endurance RPV (HALE), called the Spirit. At 85 feet, this machine will have a very much larger wing span than other contemporary RPVs, and it will have the high aspect-ratio necessary for its normal operating altitude of 52,000 feet. There are also reports that it has an absolute ceiling as high as 75,000 feet. The Spirit will have a 160 hp Teledyne Continental six-cylinder piston engine driving a large pusher propeller mounted between the twin fuselage booms. Its 1,200lb maximum payload may include fits for Elint, communications relay, targeting and Cruise Missile tracking. The Boeing Company is also reported to be working on a HALE system, again a very large wingspan machine for work at extreme altitudes. Some reports suggest that the Boeing HALE is powered by turbo-charged piston engines and that its maximum endurance may be as much as seven days in the surveillance role.

Another large Ryan machine is the Model 410 UAV (Unmanned Air Vehicle). This too is a twin-boom aircraft, this time with a wingspan of 31 feet 4 inches and a total length of 21 feet 7 inches, dimensions reminiscent of the small single-seat fighters of the Second World War. Its pusher propeller, like that of the HALE, is driven by a 160 HP Lycoming piston engine giving a top speed of 190 knots; but the most striking feature of the machine is its very large payload bay. This bay has a capacity of 24 cubic feet, which makes it possible for the Model 410, for example, to carry a payload of 300 lb. and to remain on station at a range of 1000 km for up to eight hours; or, by fitting extra fuel tanks in the bay, it can remain airborne in orbit at 30,000 ft for 19 hours.

The machine has a conventional tricycle undercarriage and takes off from prepared surfaces, though it also has a good rough field performance. It can make use of the Instrument Landing System (ILS) for recovery to airbases. At the normal gross weight of 1600 lb, the take-off run is 750 ft and, once airborne, the aircraft is controlled by a pre-set programme. Navigation is based on an inertial system, updated by a Global Positioning System receiver. This system, when in service, will overcome virtually all of the problems of inaccuracy that have hitherto plagued long-range unmanned aircraft, by making use of satellites that will give constant fixes down to a tolerance of a few feet over the surface of the earth.

The pre-set flight profile for the mission in the Model 410 can be re-programmed in flight by the two-man crew of the ground control centre (GCC) by means of an on-board computer, which links the navigation system and the autopilot as well as the controls for whichever mission sensors are carried. These sensors can be Forward-Looking Infra Red (FLIR) imaging, TV, or the sideways-looking radar planned for later versions of the basic Model 410. Plans for these more advanced vehicles include an improved engine and an extended mainplane, which together will raise the operational ceiling from the present 15,000 feet to that of perhaps 45,000 feet, and at the same time allow the maximum weight at take-off to be increased to 2400 lb. Additional fuel will be available in extra tanks fitted near the wing roots, and an endurance of 80 hours with a payload of 100 lb is then claimed to be feasible. Like most unmanned aircraft, Model 410 is not cheap and, according to one estimate, the cost of a whole system for use in the field, including six to eight aircraft, their support, FLIR and TV sensors and the necessary secure date link is likely to be somewhere between $10 million and $18 million.

Another significant system, this time one that has been operational in its original versions since about 1983 when it was deployed by the Royal Thai Air Force for surveillance work over the borders of that country, is the R4E-40 Skyeye (Figure 10.5). This project began as a development of the Aquila unmanned aircraft, which was designed and built by the Development Sciences Company, an American concern, for Lockheed in the late 1970s.

In the Skyeye project, the mainplane of the basic Aquila was extended, the fuselage deepened and a tailplane mounted on twin-booms was added to what had been a tail-less aircraft. Finally, the original engine was replaced by a 30 HP Kawasaki motor, originally designed for use on snow-mobile vehicles, driving a pusher propeller mounted between the fuselage booms. The result was the first version of Skyeye, the R4E-30. With an uprated engine, the R4E-40 model was later

Fig. 10.5. R4E-40 SKYEYE. (*Photo: Development Sciences (Astronics Division of Lear Siegler Inc.*))

produced, followed by the -50 version which has an extended mainplane and is equipped with a Teledyne 50 HP rotary engine driving a four-bladed wooden propeller.

Early versions of Skyeye carried daylight TV cameras and 35 mm daylight reconnaissance cameras, though later an infra-red camera was fitted so as to give a basic day/night capability. Payloads can now include a Xybion daylight TV camera, or a Honeywell FLIR system with fields of view that can be extended from 3 to 30 degrees. Alternatively the R4E-50 can carry a Texas Instruments IR line-scanner, a 70 mm focal length reconnaissance camera or Vinten panoramic cameras to give extra-wide terrain coverage. In the electronic warfare role, Skyeye can accept direction-finding sensors to plot radar and communications emissions, and a communications jammer.

Skyeye is not a small aircraft. It has a wingspan of 20 feet in the latest R4E-50 version, a length of 14 foot eight inches and a maximum weight at take-off of 680 lb. It has a top speed of 120 knots, a service ceiling of better than 20,000 feet and an endurance of up to 10 hours depending on the payload, which can be a maximum of 140 lb.

In operation, Skyeye is rail-launched and controlled by an autopilot manufactured by Lear Siegler, the company which had meanwhile absorbed the original constructor, Development Sciences. This autopilot is linked to an on-board waypoint navigation system which will be capable of update by the Global Positioning System. The computer system of Skyeye can store up to a total of 256 waypoints, and these are used to pre-programme in-flight changes such as those of heading, height and speed, and they can also be used to store commands for the on-board sensors.

There is in addition a ground control facility which offers two other options. When Skyeye is operated within line-of-sight ranges, continuous position updates are fed to the vehicle by means of a data-link, while the same link can transmit sensor images and status reports from the aircraft to the two-man ground control station. In the second option, Skyeye can accept revisions to its pre-programmed flight profile at longer ranges, or it can be directly and manually operated from the GCS. Skyeye is thus a drone with override facilities that can give it all the characteristics of an RPV.

Original versions of Skyeye were recovered at the end of their mission by means of a 50 foot diameter parafoil, that is to say a parachute with aerodynamic qualities more usually associated with an aerofoil, and by means of this device the aircraft could be brought down at a forward speed of as little as 20 knots to land on its retractable shock-absorbent skid. Alternatively, it could be fitted with a 42 foot diameter conventional parachute for vertical recovery if the terrain was so broken that even a low forward speed was undesirable.

The later versions of the aircraft can be landed by day or by night using the FLIR system or the on-board TV to fly the machine down an approach path by remote control. The controller adjusts engine power to give the correct glidepath and holds the aircraft level in roll, while the autopilot adjusts the pitch angle to control airspeed. The engine is cut off just before or just after landing, depending upon the particular model of the R4E.

The cost of a complete system has not been publicly revealed, but Developmental Sciences have been quoted as saying that a set of six aircraft would put the price at around $10 million to $15 million, the exact cost depending on the types of sensors

FIG. 10.6. AGM-136A Tacit Rainbow. (*Photo: Northrop Corp.*)

supplied and on the options made available to the ground controllers. It will be noted that this price is in the same range as that quoted above for the Teledyne Ryan Model 410, and seems therefore to be a reasonably accurate assessment.

In the role of defence suppression, some details have become available of Tacit Rainbow, a vehicle based on the Northrop AGM-136A (Figure 10.6). This is a new design of Williams International engine. The aircraft has pivotting wings for stowage, folding tailplanes, a fixed dorsal fin and a pop-out ventrical fin. It is about 250 centimetres in length and is designed to be air-launched from the bomb-bay of aircraft such as the B-52 after its computer is provided with the approximate location of the emitting target. The drone then flies at high sub-sonic speed to locate and to identify the emitter, adopting a loiter pattern if the target shuts down, and resuming its approach when the target resumes transmissions.

A ground-based version of Tacit Rainbow is also now in prospect, and this model would be launched from the United States Army Multiple Launch Rocket System (MLRS). In this role, the weapon would be an invaluable force-multiplier since it would neutralise enemy air defence radars in the forward areas without diminishing the payload of attack aircraft.

The Tacit Rainbow fit may also be mounted in the Boeing private venture, Brave 3000. This machine has a shorter range than the Northrop 136A and it has a lower air-speed; but it has the advantages that it is smaller, cheaper and can still be air launched or launched from the MLRS. Brave 2000, an earlier version of the 3000 Model is also a candidate for the defence suppression role, this time equipped with Pave Cricket, a loitering jamming system rather than an attack weapon.

Fig. 10.7. Launch of Canadair CL-227 Sentinel Air Vehicle. (*Photo: Canadair*)

Other recent or current programmes that should be mentioned because they appear to be making good progress include the Canadair-Dornier AN/USD-502, the Canadair Sentinel (Figure 10.7), the Ferranti Firebird and the Italian Mirach 100 model. All these unmanned aircraft are RPVs with the exception of the AN/USD-502, and all, except the Mirach 100, are surveillance and reconnaissance vehicles. Only in the Mirach is any prospect of a weapons role claimed by the manufacturer, and even in this aircraft the potential seems so far not to have been demonstrated.

Numerous other projects are at the design or experimental stages including the recoverable battlefield unmanned aircraft by Boeing Vertol, a medium range RPV (MR-RPV) at present under competitive tender by Beechcraft/Martin Marietta, Meteor SpA/Pacific Aerosystems and Northrop for the US Navy. This aircraft is intended to be a maritime surveillance platform with a range of about 650 km. The same system may become the basis of an Unmanned Air Reconnaissance System (UARS) for the USAF which is planned to enter service in the mid-1990s. This vehicle will carry thermal imagery reconnaissance devices as well as high resolution electro-optical systems, together known as the Advanced Tactical Air Reconnaissance System (ATARS). Finally, there are two vertical take-off and landing unmanned aircraft in prospect, one by Bell/Boeing, the Pointer; and the other by Grumman. Both are in a very early stage of development, and it remains to be seen whether the added complication of putting a VTOL capability into unmanned aircraft is in fact a cost-effective improvement to what was always intended to be a relatively inexpensive way of putting weapons and other systems into the air.

11

The Future of Unmanned Aircraft

Historically, unmanned military aircraft have been employed successfully in at least five sets of circumstances. First, as a deliberately indiscriminate weapon employed against civilian targets during the German V1 campaign against Britain in 1944. Second, as a weapon for use against point targets such as ships and bridges in the Second World War and later in Korea. Third, in circumstances of political hostility but without military confrontation, as was demonstrated by the American use of drones and RPVs over North Vietnam and China in the 1960s and 1970s. Fourth, militarily in conditions of politically limited war, as seen over Vietnam in the late 1960s and early 1970s. And, finally, in all-out war, for example during the Israeli operations over the Bekaa Valley in 1982. That limited experience, together with some indication of the influence of technological developments, should make it possible to give a tentative forecast about the future of unmanned aircraft.

Clearly, in many situations of confrontation short of conflict, drones and RPVs will continue to fulfil surveillance roles with unique potential for success. Their relatively low cost and the modest political embarrassment likely to be caused by their loss, seems to make them irreplaceable save by satellite operations. Since satellites are so very expensive, both in system costs and in the cost of launch, unmanned aircraft for surveillance are likely to have particular appeal to second-rank powers.

In conditions of actual combat, however, particularly in major war, the outlook for unmanned aircraft is far more complex. The most important factors will now be discussed, and since the characteristics of the two types of unmanned aircraft can be so dissimilar, drones and RPVs will be dealt with separately.

Drones

As has been pointed out, one of the principal attractions of drones to the military planner is their relatively small size and simple construction. The absence of a crew makes unnecessary a wide span of crew support equipment such as ejection seats, parachutes and survival equipment, manual controls, cockpit and canopy structures with their de-icing equipment, environmental control, filters, oxygen equipment, radios, and interface systems, such as instruments between system and crew, as well as the weight and space represented by the fully-kitted crew members themselves. By removing all these features, the designer is able to reduce not only the scale and complexity of the aircraft, but he can also reduce the size of the engine and the amount of fuel needed for the mission.

This downward spiral in complexity and cost is the direct and welcome reverse of the problem facing the designer of conventional manned aircraft. What is more, it can be accelerated, if the survival features in terms of the aeronautical performance usually found in conventional aircraft are also omitted. If, for example, a supersonic dash capability is dispensed with, then drones take another step down the spiral of complexity. And since the vehicle itself is now becoming so small that its very modest signature is itself the principal feature on which its ability to penetrate defences depends, there is little to be gained by fitting any self defence devices beyond, perhaps, a rudimentary capability to dispense chaff or small infra-red decoys, lest the spiral of complexity and size reverses and begins to climb upwards once more. There will, however, be attractions in adopting stealth technology measures, described later, in order to further to reduce the signature of the aircraft.

Such simple, small and relatively inexpensive machines clearly hold very considerable attractions, particularly in the reconnaissance role, for example. But there are also serious weaknesses. Whereas a crew is able to monitor, adapt and improvise by using the available systems of an aircraft in flight, with drones the opportunity will be there for an opponent to intervene—particularly with EW equipment—and not only to disrupt key parts of the system but also to inhibit the ability of the platform as a whole to react to that kind of operational degradation. In short, if the opponent can exploit a key component of the system, then the system can be made to enter a self-destructive cycle.

Against this, the likely use of large numbers of drones and the considerable potential for the employment of numerous, small and inexpensive decoys means that drones can be expected to have high utility in the circumstances of modern air-land warfare, particularly where they are employed in conjunction with, and more specifically in support of, manned aircraft. Their value as decoys, as triggers that expose enemy defence systems such as radar, as reconnaissance vehicles and in some circumstances as autonomous weapons systems seems certain to ensure them a significant place in the armouries of advanced air forces.

If an attack drone can survive the opposing defences, then it will be capable of accuracies as low as tens of metres at the target. This, in the case of all but the very hardest assets, such as underground bunkers or missile sites, will be adequate for a system armed with a relatively small yield nuclear warhead. If, however, the missile is to carry a conventional payload, then either the target must be an extensive one, the most obvious example being an airfield, or, if it is a small target, then the missile must be equipped with some form of terminal homing.

Against a target that is emitting heat, the solution for terminal homing is already available in infra-red seeker heads; and advances in thermal-imaging make this another important area for future developments. In the case of targets emitting radio or radar transmissions, again the problem is technically a simple one to resolve. One difficulty arises when tactics are added to technology and, for example, the target radar simply switches off. It is true that the object of the mission has thereby been achieved, since the radar has ceased to operate. But it is a simple matter to give the attacking drone the ability to loiter, and miniaturised electronic memories are already available to be fitted to anti-radiation warheads, so that each time the ground radar transmits, the missile will approach more closely to the source of the emissions as indeed some of the present more advanced drones can be programmed to do.

Against a non-emitting target, such as a building or a hardened aircraft shelter, an attacking drone will need to carry some kind of image-matching TV, IR or thermal-imagery device. These represent another expensive complexity and one that may be affected by unfavourable weather, as well as by inexpensive counter-measures, including such simple ones as smoke. These uncertainties tend to suggest that the expense of conventionally-armed but very complex drones, such as terminally guided cruise missiles, is likely to be justified only against targets of prime importance. Even at modest ranges, because the payload of a present-day cruise missile is likely to remain at a maximum of around 1200lb, the targeting will have to be highly selective. At longer ranges, not only is the en-route attrition in the face of enemy defences likely to be higher, but payload will have to be traded for extra fuel, and the cost-effectiveness of conventionally-armed cruise missiles against distant targets thus seems at the very least highly questionable.

Mobile targets will present much greater difficulties, but heightened capabilities in electronic intelligence, in optics, in conventional reconnaissance for example by high-flying aircraft, and the advent of real-time all-weather surveillance satellites mean that a very accurate and virtually instantaneous picture of opposing deployments will be made available to military commanders. This will mean that drones can be dispatched to the area of combat in which their intervention is required, and developments now in train seem likely to mean that the drone will be able, by target-imagery matching, to identify and to attack the mobile targets.

But it is important to stress that all these refinements, whether employed against static or mobile targets, clearly imply very significant steps back up the spiral of complexity, cost and in some cases the size of what began as a very simple unmanned system. A drone with the kind of capabilities just described would need to carry equipment that would enable it to fulfil as many as seven or eight separate functions; automated surveillance; target acquisition, weapon allocation, mid-course navigation or guidance, munition release and in-flight guidance in the case of autonomous sub-munitions, and terminal guidance and homing to the target. And it must be stressed that if the drone is to be successful, then all the layers of this complex programme have to be not only technically reliable, but they must be operationally robust in the face of explicit and close-range attempts by the defence to disrupt them. The future use of drones for anything but the less demanding roles will thus require fine judgement between complexity of the systems on the one hand, and the willingness of the command authorities to sacrifice considerable numbers of them in combat on the other.

RPVs

In the case of remotely piloted air vehicles, as opposed to drones, there are particular advantages but there are also new challenges, both for the designer and for the operational commander. For the RPV to operate with the effectiveness likely to be required in a modern combat environment, it will be necessary to give it at least four essential characteristics. First, all or most of the technical sensors of the manned aircraft will be needed as well as sensors to replace human vision. Second, it will be essential to have reliable communication systems that will transmit all those stimuli back to a distant operator. Third, a skilled operator will be needed who can exploit fully the qualities of the machine he is controlling, including its aerodynamic and manoeuvering characteristics. And fourth, communications systems forward to the RPV must transmit faithfully each of those reactions so as to activate the controls and equipment of the vehicle. And all this has to be accomplished in circumstances of chaos and confusion, and in a hostile operational environment against an opponent determined to disrupt or destroy critical components of the RPV's systems.

Not only that, but in operations we can expect that the RPV will be moving progressively out of the airspace in which the controller can apply his judgement to the safe progress of the aircraft, and progressively deeper into the airspace in which a skilful opponent can increasingly apply his judgement to its destruction. If the defence can exploit even a single key feature of the complex control arrays of the RPV, then here, as in the drone, the machine is likely to enter a self-destructive spiral of disabilities in a manner that an on-board crew would very often be able to prevent by judgement and improvisation.

There are also other problems to be overcome. To take for example the attack role: when the RPV reaches the target area, it has to deliver its weapons either by penetrating the dense terminal defences itself, or by using yet another link to enable the ground controller to guide a missile from the vehicle down to a target. At this point even a smoke-screen might give the remote pilot a few problems, yet the RPV and its links must have the ability to deal with these and with many other natural and contrived difficulties and obstacles.

At the same time it is clear that RPVs can offer some very clear advantages. One is that their manoeuvrability is not constrained by the frailty of the human body, and 'g' limits matter only in terms of aircraft structures. An RPV may be able to outrun an attack by manned aircraft or it may be able to evade interception altogether. It could even, in terms of 'g' loadings, out-manoeuvre a manned fighter; but what is best called the 'situational awareness' of an on-board crew in these circumstances, that is to say their on the spot ability to monitor and to react to everything around them, can never be replaced by remotely monitored sensors. The practical advantages of the manned machine are thus likely to remain overwhelming, certainly in terms of one-on-one engagements. The essential combat difference is that an RPV is a weapon or a weapon platform, whereas a manned aircraft is a *fighting* platform.

A second advantage of RPVs is that, as in the case of drones, the absence of a crew means that a great deal of space and weight in the aircraft can be saved, and combined with a continuing trend of miniaturisation in electronic and other components as well as in power sources, the RPV can be made small and much cheaper. It thus becomes possible either to evade the opposing defences by making the RPV so small and so silent that it is virtually invisible, or by using large numbers of expendable RPVs to saturate the defences to such an extent that some of these unmanned aircraft are certain to penetrate to their targets. The difficulty in miniaturising the RPV, however, is that it will then be so small that it is unable, with two exceptions, to carry a useful payload. One exception will be that of a small nuclear warhead; the other and more likely payload is that of a lightweight reconnaissance pack, as has been discussed when dealing with specific unmanned systems.

Thus, as with drones, both theory and practice suggest that RPVs will have a place in air operations of the future. The fact the RPVs are by definition more complex than drones and therefore place heavier demands on resources, both human and material, is outweighed by their wider range of potential. Drones and RPVs can both be seen to lack many of the wider attributes of manned aircraft, but they are relatively simple and inexpensive to the extent that in extreme cases they can be employed to overwhelm opposing defences by sheer weight of numbers, an option which in modern warfare is highly unlikely to be available for conventional manned aircraft.

Emerging Technology

One particularly important field for the future of unmanned aircraft is the likely impact of emerging technology. At the general level, technology is likely to be engaged to drive down the total cost of unmanned aircraft in the inventory. Here a great deal can be done by improving reliability, perhaps, though not necessarily, by accepting some increase in unit costs, but at the same time reducing the numbers of aircraft required to complete a given mission. Second, improved miniaturised engines and new fuels can be expected to decrease the power plant/payload ratio making it possible to carry more or better capabilities such as ECM fits for a given size of unmanned aircraft, or to carry the same fit in a smaller machine.

Next, advances in infra-red detector design seem likely to produce important operational improvements. In particular, the number of IR detector elements that can be fitted within an IR seeker head is being dramatically increased, and this gives three advantages. The resolution is improved, so that better surveillance and more detailed targeting will be possible; the field of view is increased with obvious advantages for reconnaissance and target acquisition; and the sensitivity of the seeker is enhanced, increasing its range by, perhaps, as much as a factor of two and giving better effectiveness in poor atmospheric conditions.

Fourth, and particularly important for future attack versions of unmanned aircraft, improvements in millimetre-wave radar are likely to be very significant. The high frequencies involved have three main implications. First, since the size of the radar is directly related to the wave length, a radar fit carried by an unmanned aircraft can be much smaller; second, because high frequencies have narrow beam widths, they are far less easy for opposing defences to jam; but third, higher frequencies give a narrower beam width which improves the discrimination of the radar and its ability to detect smaller targets—a consequence that can work for and against unmanned machines.

Next, and important for many aspects of the control and operation of unmanned aircraft, as well as in weapons systems generally, are the continuing trends in micro-miniaturisation of electronics and the striking increases in computational densities that have been produced over recent years. In the mid 1970s, for example, it was possible to fit about 1000 gate-arrays or the equivalent of seven transistors into a device one quarter of an inch square. By the early 1980s, the capacity had been increased by a factor of four, and by 1985 a device only one third larger could hold no fewer than 19,000 gate-arrays. In the last decade, computing power, using these and other devices, has increased by a factor of ten and the volume required has been reduced by a factor of six. This continuing process of increasing computational density clearly has very important implications for the operational functions of future unmanned aircraft, and in particular for the physical size of the payload and ultimately for the aircraft itself. This is likely to mean that unmanned aircraft in roles such as surveillance will have a good chance of escaping detection and engagement and that even if they are acquired by opposing weapon systems, the relatively high cost of their destruction would be justified only by the certainty that the target was indeed a reconnaissance machine and not a decoy.

The other significant field is that of stealth technology, and some discussion of this subject is essential to any discussion of the important part that stealth as a whole seems likely to play in the future of air warfare in general and in terms of unmanned aircraft in particular.

Stealth Techniques

Many modern weapon systems, and most air defence systems, depend for their accuracy on exploiting what are called the signatures of a target. These signatures can take the form of infra-red emmissions caused by sources such as engines, or they can be light reflections or noise. For air operations, the most important signature is that derived from radar reflectivity. If an aircraft is to fly undetected, then all its potential signatures must be reduced as far as possible. Ideally, they should be suppressed altogether. But above all its radar signature must be brought to an absolute minimum if the aircraft is to be given the characteristics that will enable it to operate with stealth in a hostile environment.

Radar beams have properties similar to those of light, but there are important differences. The most important of these is that light energy has a very short wave length and, because most surfaces appear rough to those waves, the light is scattered by the illuminated object. But because radar wavelengths are long, most synthetic surfaces appear smooth to the radar energy and a concentrated reflection results. It is this property that makes it possible to detect targets such as aircraft at very long ranges.

The comparatively small size of unmanned aircraft usually means a less prominent radar return, and this contributes to the characteristics of stealth as they apply to these weapons. But the amount of radar energy reflected back from a radar-illuminated target depends only partly on the size of the target. It depends more crucially on the specular reflection of the main radar lobe. There is a standard way of measuring this, known as the radar cross-section (RCS). RCS is measured by calculating the amount of radar energy reflected by a target back to the observer and then calculating the size of a sphere that would reflect the same amount of radar energy. The area of a disc of the same diameter is then called the RCS.

It is the efficiency of an object in reflecting radar energy rather than its physical size that determines its RCS. For example, a square plate 10 centimetres by 10 centimetres has a physical area of .01 square metres. But mounted at right angles to a radar beam, the same plate will have an RCS of 1 square metre, or 100 times as large. The conclusion from all this is that, in order to confer stealth characteristics on an unmanned aircraft, the same care in design will be needed as in the case of a manned machine, despite the relatively small size of unmanned vehicles.

For example, one of the principal radar-reflecting characteristics of aircraft design lies in the flat surfaces built at right angles to each other at the wing roots, on the empennage and at the attachment points of external items such as weapon pylons. These right-angled features act as highly efficient reflectors that direct radar straight back to its source. They must therefore be obviated as far as possible in the design of even very small aircraft.

Another important contribution to high RCS values is made by cavity features on aircraft, notably the engine intakes, the jet pipe and, on conventional aircraft, the cockpit. Intakes offer particular difficulties, since an efficient engine intake is almost by definition an equally efficient conduit for radar energy, which is then reflected back by the mass of the engine. Not only that, but the radar reflection can be given a characteristic beat by rotating compressor blades in turbo-jet and fan-jet engines. These can actually lead to aircraft identification with the aid of computers fitted to modern radars such as the Hughes APG-70 and 71. Some improvements in the RCS features of engine inlets and exhausts can, however, be made by sacrificing a degree of engine efficiency and by employing longer inlet and exhaust conduits. With modern engine technologies, particularly those applied to unmanned aircraft, which do not need high manoeuverability or supersonic dash capabilities, this loss of efficiency is usually acceptable.

The cockpit of manned aircraft presents another difficult challenge to the designer, but the problem clearly does not arise with unmanned vehicles, and the technical solutions of coating cockpit transparencies with substances such as indium-tin oxide, so as to permit over ninety-five per cent of light to pass through but inhibit radar rays from passing into the cockpit, are not required. Thus, detailed design may be able to eliminate many areas of high RCS, and at these lower levels of radar reflection another important contribution can be made to stealth features by the use of special materials. Structural materials based on glass and ceramics, such as fibreglass, are almost completely transparent or dielectric to radar waves, and some of these dielectric materials can be used for aircraft structures. It should be noted that their use does not necessarily mean a low RCS since the dielectric may simply allow radar waves through to be reflected from major components such as the engine and back through the material to the radar receiver. But another attribute of dielectric materials is that they can refract radar waves, just as glass or water will refract light waves. Carefully used in aircraft structures, dielectric materials can be employed to distort radar waves and thus effectively to reduce the size of the radar reflection.

Another family of materials with valuable properties in reducing RCS is that of radar absorbent materials (RAM). Each type of RAM material absorbs some radar wavelengths better than others and, because the radar waves are absorbed only gradually, the degree of absorption depends upon the depth of materials used. The efficiency of absorption also depends upon the angle of reception, so that a thin and therefore lightweight layer of RAM will be effective only against one radar wave band or at one angle.

Modern RAMs are therefore usually compound or sandwich structures, made up of different materials so as to give a wider spectrum of effect. Some of the materials in these compounds include carbon, the various ferrites and a plastic called melamine. Carbon fibre or graphite materials are particularly suitable, since these are the only non-metallic and non-conducting material that have so far proved suitable for use in the primary structures of modern combat aircraft. But although virtually none of the various RAM materials are suitable for heavy duty aircraft structures on their own, nevertheless some components on conventional aircraft, such as panels, can be made from them. They are particularly useful on structures such as those of unmanned aircraft, which are not normally subjected to high aerodynamic stress.

Because of the vital part that radar plays in air operations, the importance of RCS has been stressed. But it is not the only aircraft signature that must be minimised in the search for stealth. Another very important observable is that produced by the avionics systems of aircraft, and in particular by their radar emissions.

Of almost equal importance to the radar returns of an aircraft and to the on-board electronic emissions, is the Infra-Red signature. Like radar, the IR spectrum also makes it possible to detect aircraft and other targets beyond visual range, and it is this IR spectrum on which many weapons rely for homing-guidance to their target. The main IR signature of an aircraft is usually produced by the extreme heat from the engine exhaust, but there is also the heat from the bulk of metal in the engine itself to be taken into account. Since all objects above the temperature of absolute zero radiate a measurable amount of heat, there is even an observable signature from the heat of the aircraft structure itself. This weaker but broader IR signature from the structure of an aircraft as a whole is becoming more important as thermal imaging devices become more efficient.

It is not possible to eliminate this signature altogether. However, in future stealth aircraft it may be possible to reduce the surface temperature of the airframe, perhaps using the aircraft fuel as a heat sink, so that it would absorb the two most prominent IR bands of radiation, leaving the less visible ones to be absorbed by the atmosphere, and thus minimising the vulnerability to detection by equipment operating on these wavelengths. In the case of small unmanned aircraft, however, this seems to imply further weight and perhaps represents a less satisfactory solution than is the case with manned machines.

Finally, there are the aircraft signatures caused by aircraft noise and by the visibility of an aircraft both to the human eye and to electro-optical systems. Various technical measures can be taken to reduce the noise of jet engines. In the case of unmanned aircraft in particular they are not inconsistent with the measures that are effective in reducing RCS and IR signatures. Some noise will, however, always remain and only small and lower powered propeller driven aircraft are likely to offer extremely low acoustic signatures. Many small drones and RPVs take advantage of this factor.

Using the optical spectrum to detect and engage targets takes us back to the fundamentals of warfare, and to the use of night and bad weather to evade opposing defences. Here, some assistance can be offered by technology, either in terms of aircraft configuration, an approach that is again consistent with the search for low RCS signatures for the operation of RPVs and drones, or in terms of various camouflage techniques, including special surface finishes designed to reduce the contrast of an aircraft against the sky.

A SYNTHESIS OF SYSTEMS

It thus seems clear that in the technical sense there is considerable future potential for the development of military aircraft in general, and for small unmanned aircraft in particular. Two fields of technology have been stressed here as particularly significant, those of micro-miniaturisation and of stealth techniques, and they seem likely to play a formative role in deciding the place of unmanned aircraft in the broader spectrum of air power.

Although it is clear that comparatively little effort is at present being devoted by major air forces to the development of unmanned aircraft, it is equally clear that these machines are likely to play a significant, if limited, part in future confrontations, crises and war. Quite apart from the obvious and proven value of unmanned aircraft in the surveillance and reconnaissance role, the trends in technology suggest that if the balance between defence techniques and attack techniques continue their present pattern of pendulum-like shifts, then unmanned aircraft will have considerable utility in at least four other types of mission.

First, in the ECM role, micro-miniaturisation of comparatively powerful electronic emitters means that unmanned aircraft will be effective as jammers against many classes of radar emitter. Passive ECM machines will be able to complement that active role by detecting and locating hostile transmitters, reporting the data back to ground stations or, more significantly, reporting it to airborne attack aircraft so that near real-time hard kills can be scored.

Second, hard kills should continue to be possible through direct attack by unmanned aircraft. Even using current technology, drones can be launched and programmed to make their own way to a target and to attack it without further intervention by a controller. For less prominent targets and for mobile targets, RPVs can be guided to the required area, there to launch weapons on command once the targets have been acquired by the distant operator.

Third, there is the stand-off attack mission. The tendency in air power concepts over the past few decades has been to emphasise the potential to evade efficient defences by employing air-launched stand-off weapons. Particularly in the theatre land-air battle, this combination employs all the advantages of the manned platform that were discussed earlier to penetrate hostile airspace and to avoid or to counter en-route defences up to the point at which the dense, dedicated, and perhaps lethal defences of key targets would be encountered. From that point on, the advantages of the missile, usually some form of unmanned aircraft, can be exploited.

Such stand-off weapons will not be inexpensive, and nor will they provide a sufficient answer to all the problems of the land-air battle. They will need to be used judiciously so as to neutralise the key features of opposing air defences and to exploit critical weaknesses in ground-force arrays. And nor will they be a substitute for the firepower that will also be needed in order to consolidate the military paralysis induced by the selective employment of high technology weapons. In very many operational circumstances, numbers and sheer weight of firepower are likely to remain a vital factor.

Fourth, and of very real significance for the future, there is a heightened potential for progress in that important factor of war, deception. This is because stealth technology, while certainly unable to erase all the signatures of an aircraft, can at least greatly reduce them, and particularly the RCS. At the same time, it is a simple matter to *add* RCS enhancing measures to relatively inexpensive unmanned aircraft. Thus it is possible to envision attack packages that would include not only decoys of this kind, but also other types of unmanned aircraft that would have passive or active roles in the assault. The problems confronting the defence would be considerable. Even if the defence proved able to distinguish unmanned aircraft, it would still be extremely difficult to distinguish pure decoys from decoy-like machines that actually carried operational support capabilities such as ECM fits.

Thus, the notion, once prevalent, that unmanned aircraft were a challenge to conventional machines and would one day replace them, should be replaced by an acceptance that both types of aircraft have a part to play in modern air warfare, and that unmanned aircraft, far from replacing manned versions are more likely in the future to act in their direct support. Meanwhile, the essential need to bring situational awareness and operational judgement to the scene of confused combat, means that manned aircraft are likely to remain the principal asset in the exercise of air power.

Self-Test Questions

Chapter 1   Origins

1. When did the first live experiments with unmanned aircraft take place in the United Kingdom?
2. What was the Kettering Bug?
3. What was the Larynx aircraft, and how did it get its name?
4. What was the Fairey Queen, and what did experiments in the Mediterranean in 1933 demonstrate?

Chapter 2   Emergence—The V1 Weapon

5. What was the world's first successful operational cruise missile?
6. What was the key technical innovation that led to the development of the German V1 weapon?
7. Why was the inaccuracy of the V1 flying bomb an asset rather than a liability?
8. What were the main problems facing the British defences?
9. What steps did the German High Command take to monitor the success of their offensive?
10. And what measures did British Military Intelligence take to deceive the enemy?
11. Describe the main effects of the V1 campaign on the British war effort.
12. Say approximately how many V1s were launched, and how many reached the London Civil Defence Region.
13. How many casualties were caused in Britain by the campaign, and how do the numbers compare with the total casualties sustained in Britain by bombing and by the later attacks by V2 weapons?

Chapter 3   Unmanned Aircraft at War

14. List the various means by which German glide-bombs were guided in the Second World War.
15. What successes did these glide-bombs achieve in the Mediterranean theatre of war?
16. What were the imperatives that drove the Germans to devote so much ingenuity and so many scarce resources to programmes for experimental systems?
17. Why did the United States Army Air Corps show an interest in glide-bombs during 1944?
18. What weapons guidance systems were employed by the USAAC in their glide-bombs?
19. What was Aphrodite?

Chapter 4   The Missile Age

21. What factors discouraged the development of United States Navy unmanned aircraft for attack missions in the early years of the Second World War?

22. What development rekindled American interest in unmanned aircraft towards the end of the Second World War, and what was the immediate result?
23. What was the essential difference between the German V1 cruise missile and the American JB-2 machine?
24. Describe the main features and the main operational weaknesses of Snark.
25. Why was the Navaho programme cancelled?

Chapter 5   More Second Generation Cruise Missiles

26. Which system did Matador employ to overcome the problem of long-range accuracy? Describe its characteristics and the difficulties that limited its usefulness.
27. Why was the Regulus programme abandoned?
28. What factors led to the demise of what has been described in Chapter 5 as the second generation cruise missiles?

Chapter 6   Towards Third Generation Cruise Missiles

29. In October 1953, the balance of advantage between early cruise missiles and ICBMs changed decisively in favour of the latter. What was the new factor?
30. Although ICBMs took a leading position in US developments of strategic systems during the 1950s, two other roles remained to unmanned aircraft. What were they?
31. What event in the Middle East led to renewed United States interest in cruise missiles?
32. Which two United States short-range cruise missile systems survived beyond the early 1970s?
33. Describe the British cruise missile that was deployed with Victor and Vulcan bombers.
34. On what role did the Soviet programme for cruise missile concentrate in the 1950s and 1960s, and why?
35. Say what you know about the AS-15 cruise missile.

Chapter 7   Operational Experience with Unmanned Aircraft

36. What was the origin of the American programme of unmanned aircraft developed at the time of the war in Vietnam?
37. What events in May and July 1960 accelerated the US reconnaissance drone programme?
38. Describe the mission profile of air-launched Ryan 147 unmanned aircraft as employed over China and Vietnam in the Summer of 1964.
39. What advantage was thus demonstrated in using unmanned rather than manned aircraft in this role?
40. What were the operating problems that were encountered over North Vietnam in the mid-1960s?
41. Which version of the basic Ryan 147 drone had the longest production run, and what were its characteristics?

42. Describe the main features of the Israeli Scout system.
43. Describe the part played by Israeli unmanned aircraft in the Bekaa Valley operation of 1982.

Chapter 8   United States Cruise Missiles Revived

44. What was the gap in strategic systems that the United States sought to exploit by developing advanced cruise missiles?
45. Three factors then gave impetus to the cruise missile programme. What were they?
46. Describe the Tercom navigation system.
47. What is DSMAC, and what is its function?
48. Describe the advances in technology that made possible advanced cruise missiles.
49. How many variants of Tomahawk were developed? What were their roles?
50. What is a TEL, and what does it weigh?
51. List the arguments that favoured Ground Launched Cruise Missiles in NATO, rather than air or sea launched versions of these weapons.

Chapter 9   Concepts of Manned and Unmanned Aircraft

52. What is the Relative Price Effect, and what approximate percentage rise in the cost of defence equipment does it represent?
53. Give some illustrative figures for the cost of modern defence equipment, including unmanned aircraft.
54. In what ways is the rising cost of manned aircraft being abated?
55. Give some illustrative figures for the effectiveness of modern weapons systems as compared to those of the Second World War.
56. Discuss mobility in the context of manned and unmanned aircraft.
57. Discuss the advantage of manned and unmanned aircraft in crisis management.
58. What do you understand by role flexibility? And what is combat flexibility?

Chapter 10   Present Programmes

59. List the three roles for unmanned aircraft identified by NATO.
60. What are the roles of Phoenix?
61. Describe the principal features of Skyeye.
62. Describe the mode of operation of Acquila.

Chapter 11   Future of Unmanned Aircraft

63. Why can drones be made to be so much smaller than manned aircraft?
64. List the main advantages and disadvantages of drones.
65. What essential characteristics must be designed into an RPV?
66. What are the advantages of RPVs?
67. Which emerging technologies seem most likely to play a role in the future development of unmanned aircraft?

68. What is RCS, and how is it measured?
69. Why is the IR signature of. aircraft likely to be very significant for future developments?
70. What aircraft signatures other than radar and IR are significant?
71. In what four types of mission is it suggested that unmanned aircraft will have considerable future utility?

Glossary

AA	Anti-Aircraft.
ACN	Automatic Celestial Navigation (equipment).
ALCM	Air Launched Cruise Missile.
Attack	Offensive action, but usually taken to imply the use of conventional as opposed to nuclear (strike) weapons.
ATRAN	Automatic Terrain Recognition and Navigation. Early radar map-matching navigation system used in the Matador cruise missile.
Aphrodite	Code-name for time-expired bomber aircraft used as unmanned attack weapons during the Second World War by USAAC and USN.
ARM	Anti-Radar Missile.
ATARS	Advanced Tactical Air Reconnaissance System
BKEP	Boosted Kinetic Energy Penetrator. An airfield attack munition.
BLACS	Barometric Low Altitude Control System, used in Ryan 147 RPVs.
Carpet	Second World War electronic warfare technique to counter defence radars.
C.E.P.	Circular Error Probable. The radius of a circle into which 50 per cent of aimed weapons can be expected to fall.
Chaff	Strips of radar-reflective material dispensed to simulate intended target and thus draw off defences.
Cruise Missile	Self-sustaining, air breathing aerodynamic missile.
Crossbow	Air campaign by Allies against German V1 and V2 weapons and logistics in 1944. Also name of an American decoy missile in the 1950s.
CW	Radio carrier waves.
Drone	Autonomous and automatic crew-less aircraft.
DSMAC	Digital Scene-Matching Area Correlator.
ECM	Electronic Counter-Measures.
ECCM	Electronic Counter-Counter-Measures.
ELINT	Electronic Intelligence.
ESM	Electronic Support Measures.
EW	Electronic Warfare.
Flak	Ground-based anti-aircraft guns, from German *Fliegerabwehrkannone*.
FLASH	Firebee Low-Altitude Ship-to-Ship Homing Missile.
FLIR	Forward Looking Infra Red.
GCS	Ground Control Station.
GLCM	Ground Launched Cruise Missile.
ICBM	Intercontinental Ballistic Missile.
IFF	Identification Friend or Foe.
ILS	Instrument Landing System.
IR	Infra-Red.

KG	*Kampfgruppe*; German formation nomenclature as in III KG1—*Kampfgruppe 1* of *Luftflotte III*.
Linebacker	US Code-name for air attacks against Hanoi and Haiphong.
JATO	Jet Assisted Take-off, i.e., auxiliary pods, usually small disposable rockets, to accelerate an aircraft or a missile at take-off.
MACS	Multi-Altitude Control System (for Ryan 147 RPVs).
Mandrell	Second World War anti-radar technique.
MARS	Mid-Air Retrieval System.
MCGS	Microwave Command Guidance System.
MLRS	Multi-Launch Rocket System.
MRASM	Medium Range Air-to-Surface Missile.
RAM	Radar Absorbent Material.
RCS	Radar Cross Section.
RPV	Remotedly Piloted Vehicle.
SAM	Surface-to-Air Missile.
SALT	Strategic Arms Limitation Talks.
SCAD	Subsonic Cruise Armed Decoy.
SCAM	Subsonic Cruise Attack Missile.
SCUD	Subsonic Cruise Unarmed Decoy.
Shanicle	Hyperbolic grid navigation system used in Matador cruise missile.
SLAM	Submarine Launched Attack Missile.
SLBM	Submarine Launched Ballistic Missile.
SLCM	Submarine Launched Cruise Missile.
SRAM	Short Range Attack Missile.
SSGN	Designation for nuclear-powered attack submarine armed with cruise missiles.
STAWS	Submarine Tactical Anti-Ship Weapons System.
Strike	Offensive action, but normally taken to mean the use of nuclear rather than conventional weapons.
TAAM	Tactical Airfield Attack Munition.
TASM	Tactical Anti-Ship Missile.
TEL	Transporter-Erector-Launcher; vehicle used to transport and launch GLCMs.

Bibliography

ANDERTON, DAVID A. *B-29 Superfortress at War*, Ian Allen Ltd, 1978.

BENEKE and QUICK. *History of German Guided Missiles*, Agard, 1957.

BERGER, CARL, Editor. *The United States Air Force in South East Asia 1961–73*. Office of Air Force History, USA, 1977.

BETTS, RICHARD K, Editor. *Cruise Missiles, Technology, Strategy, Politics*, Brookings Institution, 1981.

CECIL, ROBERT CMG (Editorial Consultant). *Hitler's War Machine*. Hamlyn Publishing Group, 1975.

COLLIER, BASIL. *The Defence of the United Kingdom*, HMSO, 1957.

COLLIER, BASIL. *The Battle of the V-Weapons 1944–1945*, Hodder & Stoughton Ltd, 1964.

COOKSLEY, PETER G. *Flying Bomb*, Robert Hale Ltd, 1979.

DORNBERGER, Major General WALTER. *V2*, Hurst & Blackett Ltd, 1954.

FREEMAN, ROGER A. *The Mighty Eight, Units, Men and Machines*, MacDonald & Co Ltd, London, 1970,

FREEMAN, ROGER A. *The US Strategic Bomber*, MacDonald & Co Ltd, London, 1975.

FUTRELL, ROBERT F. *United States Air Force in Korea 1950–53*, Duell, Sloan & Pearce, New York, 1961.

GANDER, TERRY and CHAMBERLAIN, PETER. *Small Arms and Special Weapons of the Third Reich*, MacDonald & Janes Ltd, London, 1978.

GATLAND, KENNETH W. *Development of the Guided Missile*, for *Flight* by Illiffe & Sons, London, 2nd Edition, 1954.

GUNSTAN, BILL. *The Illustrated Encyclopaedia of the World's Rockets and Missiles*, Salamander Books Ltd, London, 1979.

GURNEY, Colonel GENE USAF (Retd). *Vietnam the War in the Air*, Sidgwick & Jackson Ltd, 1985.

HENSHALL, PHILIP. *Hitler's Rocket Sites*, Robert Hale Ltd, 1985.

HOGG, IAN V and KING, J B. *German and Allied Secret Weapons of World War II*, Phoebus Publishing Ltd, London, 1979.

LONGMATE, NORMAN. *The Doodlebugs: The Story of the Flying Bomb*, Hutchinson & Co Ltd, London, 1981.

LONGMATE, NORMAN. *Hitler's Rockets—The Story of the V-2s*, Hutchinson & Co Ltd, London, 1985.

MOLONEY, Brigadier C J C. *History of the Second World War. The Mediterranean and the Middle East, Vol VI, Pt 1*, HMSO, 1984.

O'BRIEN, TERENCE H. *Civil Defence*, HMSO & Longmans, Green and Co, London, 1975.

ORDWAY III, FREDERICK I and SHARPE, MITCHELL R. *The Rocket Team*, William Heineman Ltd, 1979.

PITT, BARRIE (Editor-in-Chief). *German Secret Weapons—Blueprint for Mars*, MacDonald & Co Ltd, London, 1970.

RODGERS, A L (with FOWLER I B R, GARLAND-COLLINS T K, GOULD J A, JAMES D A and ROPER W). *Brassey's Battlefield Weapons Systems & Technology, Vol VII, Surveillance and Target Acquisition Systems*, Brassey's Defence Publishers, 1983.

RUST, KEN C. *The 9th Air Force in World War 2*, Aero Publishers Inc. USA, 1967.

SCHWIEBERT, ERNEST G. *A History of the USAF Ballistic Missiles*, Frederick A Praeger Publishers, London, 1965.

SORRELS, CHARLES A. *US Cruise Missiles. Programmes, Development, Deployment and Implications for Arms Control*, Brassey's Publishers Ltd, London, 1983.

SWEETMAN, BILL. *Stealth Aircraft: Secrets of Future Airpower*, Airlife Publishing Ltd, 1986.

TAYLOR, MICHAEL J H. *Missiles of the World*, Ian Allan Ltd, 1980.

TAYLOR, JOHN W R (Editor). *Jane's Pocket Book of RPVs: Robot Aircraft Today*, MacDonald & Janes, London, 1977.

TAYLOR, JOHN W R (Editor). *Jane's Weapon's Systems*, various Editions, Jane's, London.

TAYLOR, JOHN W R (Editor). *Jane's All The World's Aircraft*, various Editions, Jane's, London.

WAGNER, WILLIAM. *Lightning Bugs and Other Reconnaissance Drones*, Aero Publishers Inc, California, 1982.

WERRELL, KENNETH P. *The Evolution of the Cruise Missile*, Air University Press, Maxwell AFB, September 1985.

YOUNG, RICHARD A. *The Flying Bomb*, Ian Allan Ltd, 1978.

Index